The Gradiva Prize

Each year a few organisations such as the Italian Psychoanalytic Society (SPI) and the Jungian Analysts hold a Congress at Lavarone, near Trento, an Alpine resort. It was here that Freud wrote his Gradiva paper. The Congress takes place at Hotel du Lac where Freud was on holiday. At the end of the Congress a jury awards a prize to the author of a book, who becomes the guest of honour and stays in Freud's room.

Franco De Masi won the first Gradiva Prize:

> This well deserved award goes to a text that successfully marries scientific rigour with accessibility. The author conveys the depth of his thinking through his simple, effective and concise prose. De Masi offers us a close reading of the most important psychoanalytic theories and his capacity to adhere to internal reality, the essence of our discipline. In so doing, he has produced a text, which elicits the affectively charged thoughtfulness, appropriate to the reader's psychic experience.
>
> De Masi treats the theme of death, whose unrelenting harshness arouses anxieties akin to a catastrophic trauma, in a clear and engaging style. "Making Death Thinkable", however, makes for a poignant read, as the author carefully shows us a way to redemption. It is not the same redemption promised by religion, but rather the consolation deriving from feeling part of humanity, which will go on living.
>
> It is possible to accept our own death as individuals by coming to terms with and integrating the legacy from the past and opening ourselves up to the possibility of investing and projecting onto other people's future lives. The future thus represents the avenue for collective reparation, through a transgenerational transmission that locates the flow of life beyond the death of the subject. This is one of the most important merits of the book, as it offers solace to the specific and novel malaise of our times.
>
> This work was also praised for its light touch, which together with its profundity leaves the reader with a sense of gratitude to the author.

Lavarone, July 12th 2003

MAKING DEATH THINKABLE

MAKING DEATH THINKABLE

A psychoanalytic contribution to the problem of the transience of life

Franco De Masi

Foreword by Paul Williams

Editorial Consultant Anthony Molino
Translated by Pina Antinucci

Free Association Books
FA^B

First published 2004
by Free Association Books
57 Warren Street W1T 5NR

© 2004 Franco De Masi

All rights reserved. No part of this publication
may be reproduced, stored in a retrieval system,
or transmitted, in any form or by any means,
without the prior permission in writing
of the publisher.

This book is sold subject to the condition
that it shall not, by way of trade or otherwise,
be lent, resold, hired out or otherwise circulated
without the publisher's prior consent in any form
other than that supplied by the publisher.

British Library Cataloguing in Publication Data
A catalogue record for this book is available from the British Library

Produced by Bookchase (UK) Ltd

ISBN 1 853437 83 2
L.D.: SE-3143-2004 in Spain
Printed by Publidisa

Publisher's Dedication

This book is dedicated to R. M. Young who founded Free Association Books in 1983. His vision and flair in the early years resulted in the publication of many books which have now become classic psychoanalytic texts, providing the inspiration and material resources for this translation.

To Paola Capozzi and Vittorio Linciardi, invaluable interlocutors in the writing of this text.

Only music illuminates, brightens and consoles us. It is not just a fragile support to hold on to. It is a faithful friend that protects and comforts and, only thanks to it, life in this world is worth living. Perhaps in heaven there will be no music. This is why we stay on this earth as long as life allows us.

P.I. Cajkovskij

Death, if that is what we want to call this unreality.
G.F.W. Hegel, *Phenomenology of the Spirit*

CONTENTS

Foreword to English Edition by Paul Williams   11
Foreword by Sergio Bordi   13

Introduction   21

PART ONE
Unthinkable Death

1 On Transience   31

2 The Denial of Time and the Myth of Immortality   34

3 Panic Attack or Imaginary Death   40

4 Psychic Strategies towards Self-Annihilation   49

5 Fear or Serenity?   65

6 Potential Self and Absence of Future   70

7 A Higher Level of Consciousness   76

8 Ivàn I'Lìc's Death   81

9 The Mid-Life Crisis   86

10 Psychoanalysis in Old Age   97

11 Death and Psychosis   104

12 An Unthinkable Event   110

13 Death: What Reparation?   119

PART TWO
The Unconscious and Death in Freud and in Melanie Klein

14 The Denial of Death   129

15 The Problem of Mourning   133

16 The Death Instinct   136

17 Melanie Klein and Innate Destructiveness   146

Bibliography   150
Index   156

FOREWORD TO THE ENGLISH TRANSLATION

This foreword will be brief, like the book to which it refers.

It will not, however, possess the depth that Franco De Masi brings to a subject that dominates life and yet receives disproportionately little consideration from psychoanalysts.

It is typical of Franco De Masi's style that he focuses unremittingly on the core elements of his subject. We have seen this time and again in his papers on psychosis, sadomasochism, perversion and so on. It is as though De Masi is acutely conscious that there is no time to waste. In these few pages he addresses the nature of death anxiety, which is ubiquitous, and makes the fundamental link between this and a failure to properly mourn. He addresses the omnipotence of fantasies of immortality and their corollary, panic attacks and imaginary death. What is striking is how widely De Masi ranges in his analytic thinking, and the facility with which he links ideas and makes valuable conceptual connections, for example between narcissism, the death instinct and addictive autoerotism. He brings vividly to life processes of psychotic regression that embrace inertia and death as defences against unbearable depression and mental pain, and of particular note is the depth of his reflections on the fear of dying versus death anxiety, which he explores from both a philosophical and a psychoanalytic perspective to try to develop our currently inadequate analytic models.

It is particularly useful in an age of pluralism that at times can resemble factionalism in psychoanalysis, that De Masi integrates with modesty and skill the theories of Freud, Klein and Winnicott in a way that allows for an articulation of the internal origins of death anxiety to be related to development and the evolution of a sense of Self within the life cycle.

Undogmatic, creative links of the kind De Masi makes are, to my mind, the stuff of the best psychoanalytic writing. Of value also is the inclusion of Bollas's development of Winnicottian thought on mourning and loss as being linked to the limitation of future developments of the Self. Winnicott's hypothesis, the fear of death and illness reactivate to the primitive terror of the disintegration of the Self, coupled with Bollas's intimations of the futurity of loss, make a compelling counterpoint to the impact of unconscious fantasy which lies at the root of self deception. De Masi also recruits Edelman, Tolstoy and Elliot Jacques to examine the vicissitudes of the development of the Self.

In the second part of the book De Masi deals with the unconscious and death in Freud and in Melanie Klein. This is an exploration of crises in mourning, of the notion of the death instinct, and of the innate destructiveness that Klein posited that lay at the root of psychopathology. It is difficult to grasp that so much ground can be covered in one small, slim volume. It is to De Masi's credit that he has elevated anxiety around death to a central place in contemporary psychoanalytic thinking.

In this sense this book is an original contribution and one that will help to generate much future scholarship.

Paul Williams
Joint Editor in Chief, International Journal of Psychoanalysis
June 2004

FOREWORD BY SERGIO BORDI

The present crisis that psychoanalysis is going through, and the decrease in interests it is experiencing, strengthen the view of those who have always regarded our discipline as a cultural phenomenon typical of a time of transition. This view is also shared by those who consider psychoanalysis to be the expression of Modernism, in its advanced state and intent on self-critique. If this is the case, our discipline seems destined to die out together with post-modernism.

These views would show as scientifically groundless the claim of Psychoanalysis to being a universally valid account of the nature and development of the mind, in health and in sickness. This criticism has further been enhanced by the critique of the philosophical premises of Realism of the last few decades. The critics of Realism emphasise that the knowing subject constructs the object of knowledge through a powerful subjective contribution. Therefore, strictly speaking, we cannot claim that we really discover the object. This statement, in fact, presupposes the existence of an objective world, independent of any human experience or thought and also that it might be possible to tell whether our statements about it are true or false, according to their correspondence to any observable fact. The ensuing conclusion is that the researchers' claims do not constitute objective truths, any more than any other belief.

As human beings' capacity to interpret reality is unlimited, an objective and universally valid truth would have very uncertain foundation, indeed. The only certainty would reside in our acceptance of the multiplicity of languages with which various eras and cultures describe the world. It is thus essential to remain deeply sceptical whenever anyone mentions identifiable and definable mental contents, or human nature as something stable and permanent. Likewise, Darwin and Freud conceptualised human nature as something little changeable in the face of variable conditions of life – or death, to address the topic of this book.

We could go into more details and define in the simplest possible way the assumptions underlying our discipline in the early days. All psychoanalysts subscribed to the concept of insight, and thought that the psychoanalytic method would enable those who underwent treatment to discover some important truths about themselves, previously hidden by repression. Nowadays that commonly held belief has been very much undermined, and consequently socioconstructivist and pragmatist currents of thought, strengthened by Ermeneutics, have presently many followers. Even the Freudian belief, originated in the Enlightenment, according to which cure and self-knowledge converge, has been eroded.

With an extremely simple and concise exposition, which conceals the depth of his thinking, Franco De Masi shows how he does not let himself be carried away with these trends. He does not believe that what he tells an anorectic patient or a sufferer of panic attacks might simply offer an alternative perspective to hold them, so that they might lead a more bearable life, but rather, he is convinced that what he communicates to them bears a relation to their internal reality. In other words, he thinks that he has a professional competence, which enables him to make some reasonably appropriate and accurate inferences about the patient's intrapsychic contents. He is also aware of his subjective involvement with his patients, who externalise their internal scenario, inevitably drawing him in. This is why when we read "the psychoanalyst should help the patient to develop his or her capacity to tolerate the thought of human transience", we soon realise that the person who states this is not afraid of being mistaken for a priest or accused of making suggestions.

The spirit that informs this long essay can be traced back to the original sources of psychoanalytic inquiry, whose guiding line was the attainment of a realistic conceptualisation of human motivation. Psychoanalytic theory located the causal forerunners of adulthood in the early years of life and provided also a potential promise of what human beings could still become, beyond the limits of their individual lives.

These boundaries, however, delineate a stopping line for us all. The harsh theme, which this book purports to investigate, is the pain ensuing from our awareness that "we owe a death" and that time is cruelly too brief to be able to give a meaning to the only life cycle available to us. This is one of the hardest and most painful themes to grapple with, as it confronts the subject with an unthinkable aspect of the self.

We are warned, straight away, that the author will refrain from commenting on the contributions from religious, philosophical and anthropological fields of enquiry, even though he acknowledges that there are many pertinent and often illuminating ones. His only frame of reference is psychoanalytic theory and his main objective is to reflect on what the most noteworthy psychoanalytic thinkers have said on the notion of death.

The biological premise constitutes an implicit assumption to the psychoanalytic discourse. As the psychoanalyst's knowledge advances within a multidisciplinary context, De Masi begins each chapter with epigraphic literary-philosophical quotations. Some of them are extraordinarily beautiful, even when the following chapter deals with the Darwinian competition amongst neurones, or with the mechanisms which regulate the death of the cells.

We often state that our body is a machine, but we do not always remember that it is a rather peculiar one. It destroys and re-creates itself incessantly, whilst its morphofunctional structure remains invariant. In each one of the hundred billion cells that make up our organism, lives the gene of death, which has the capacity to decide whether that particular cell should live or not. All of this takes place within that sidereal silence where Freud located the death instinct.

It is from here that De Masi's reflections start. He begins by reminding us of the perplexities elicited in the world of psychoanalysis when confronted with the hypothesis that, unlike the life instinct, the death instinct is not supposed to have representational derivatives. Likewise it is perplexing having to accommodate the hypothesis that the cognisance of death, even though it painfully stamps itself on the ego, when it loses the loved one, does not reach the id, which would continue, unperturbed, to weave the web of life.

Ego psychology ignored the death instinct and its opposition is summed up by Erikson's statement: "The death instinct is a magnificent contradiction in terms". The analyst who embraced it with total commitment was Melanie Klein, who, nevertheless, described its vicissitudes within the context of object relations. Her view was that the ego, present from birth, recognises the death instinct, so much so that it projects it into the breast, feeling, in turn, threatened by it. Gradually the danger of dying decreases and therefore the paranoid-schizoid position loses its primacy and the splitting between good and bad decreases as well. However, when the split off parts achieve integration, the ego acknowledges that the object of the death instinct is also the life-giving object. At this point the threat that the object might perish, carrying the ego with it, becomes acute. Thus the needs to restore the object and keep it alive gain strength.

It is not difficult to realise that within this framework the fantasy of death has its place beside the Freudian "desire". This fantasy, just as in the Bible, joins the history of humanity alongside sin, the necessity to repair it and the notion of compassion. The reference point is no longer the totem animal, the murder of the father and the origin of the Law, but rather the apotropaic ritual aiming at averting the danger that the dead return among the living or turn those who loved them into salt statues. After dwelling on some of the reasons why the Freudian hypothesis is not very plausible, De Masi concludes: "the fear of dying is ineliminable and accompanies us throughout our life". His next remark is that this fear can manifest itself as a request for help. The author thus reveals his need to come, before long, to the essential questions: how the fear of death could be explained, what factors come into play when it is excessive and uncontainable, and what factors, on the contrary, inhibit this fear or might even bring about the pleasure of self-destruction.

The book gives a special attention to this last occurrence (and this is not surprising, if one thinks about *The Sado-masochistic Perversion*, which was published a couple of years ago). Suggestive references to Martin Eden's suicide and to the classic paper by Karl Abraham on Segantini conclude these remarks.

The previous questions immediately call to mind another, very pertinent one: what childhood have these patients had? To provide an answer "the new views on real trauma", Winnicott's descriptions of the mother-infant relationship and the vicissitudes of the conflict between the libidinal self and the destructive self put forward by Rosenfeld are in turn examined.

At this point it might have been useful to give some space to the concept of reverie formulated by Bion, an author towards whom, in any case, De Masi has always shown a marked affection. According to Bion, the mother's capacity to "contain" mentally the affective state, intolerable to the infant, permits the modulation of the emotional stress, so that it makes it possible for the baby to work through it on the representational level.

Attachment theory has come to similar conclusions to Bion's, with the addition of a substantial empirical content. On the basis of these contributions, we now think that those individuals, who experience anxiety as a catastrophe, have not had adequate maternal mirroring in infancy and so are not equipped with a symbolic barrier able to contain the state of physiological disequilibrium. Therefore their ineffective strategy for affect regulation seems linked to an inadequate internal presence of that maternal mind that intuitively understands the physical stressful state and "disjoins" it, representing it as a tolerable physical state, thus facilitating the process of "mentalization".

The following chapter deals with "another occurrence, less emphasised in psychoanalytic writings, which reveals an absence of the common defences that protect us from pain and (. . .) in which the absence of the fear of death demands that we reflect on the nature of the pleasure that underlies the self-destructive movement". The author is well aware that this is a rather thorny issue, which ultimately leads to the complex question of narcissism.

As we all know, Freud stated that human beings are fundamentally narcissistic, a statement that, when we look around, does not really seem so excessive, after all. Perhaps, as a consequence of statements like these, the primacy of the psychosexual model decreased, whereas the trend, from which self-psychology originated, gained momentum. Also, the notion of object love became less clear. According to the drive theory, the object is accepted out of necessity, because the advent of the reality principle shows the inefficacy of the pleasure principle. On this basis, we can come to loving the object for what it is, whether it gratifies us or not: and this is what we are accustomed to defining as "true love". Conversely, according to the theory of narcissism, the libido is essentially hostile to the object and it is always ready to withdraw into the ego. Thus, to be able to become a love object, the object must have some qualities, which will affirm its importance for the functioning and the organisation of the ego, constituting something very similar to Kohut's self-object.

De Masi observes that the introduction of the death instinct adds further complexities to psychoanalytic theory. He also points out the contradiction present in Freud, who alternatively seems to conceptualise the death instinct as a locus of dramatic conflicts or as a quiet return to Nirvana. In reality Freud's explanatory framework was founded on the constancy principle, now outdated, whereas contemporary biology regards organisms as active entities, moving towards states of increasing complexity and coherence. Therefore hypotheses, which explain psychopathology as a regression to the state of utter intrauterine passivity, have lost their credibility. De Masi mentions them in passing and quickly discards them. However it is clear that De Masi does not wish to dwell too much upon these theoretical aspects, as he is much keener on the clinical work. In particular, he wishes to examine the treatment of those patients who do not experience the anxiety ordinarily associated with death and act against their best interest, to the point of putting their own survival in jeopardy. He reports both the cases of those who pursue a state of apparently quiet non-existence and those who exalt and idealise death in a triumphant state of intoxication.

He suggests that the pleasure of self-destruction is linked to an omnipotent fantasy with two complementary aspects: a transgressive erotization and an autoerotic withdrawal, which obliterate any mentalization and contact with the world. These hypotheses render explicit De Masi's theoretical affinity with Bion and his notions of the attacks on the perceptive apparatus and "-K" condition, whilst less relevant appear to be Rosenfeld's ideas on the competition between a destructive, narcissistic and a libidinal organisation. The latter is closely linked to the world of objects and receives the analyst's support.

If we bear in mind the "subjective forms" of experience illustrated by Winnicott, or Tustin's "varieties of autistic sensations", or Fraiberg's observations of how neglected children's *freeze*, we might be more inclined to make use of Rosenfeld's ideas. In fact, through all the defensive strategies just mentioned, the subject's main aim is to support him/herself in a state of total self-regulation and avoid any contact with the other. In such a condition, any external intervention is experienced as a highly traumatic intrusion: something similar to what we all feel when we are listening to a quartet and are assaulted by the neighbour's radio kept at high volume.

These conditions, as well as alexithymia, are clinically very interesting because they are consistent with the findings of infant research on the mechanisms which allow the child to employ cognitive processes in order to modulate states of increasing emotional intensity and, in turn, to utilise its affects to extend its cognitive information.

Examining cases of pathological dwelling on death, understandably brings De Masi to talk about the experience of facing, within oneself, the prospect of the end of life. At this point, quite appropriately, his discourse acquires a more philosophical breadth. With the "mid life crisis", these experiences become more frequent. They manifest themselves when the part of us in contact with others allows the other, care-taking part, to remind ourselves how far we have gone in the journey of our life. We usually allow this part to claim our attention and entertain us in a dialogue vaguely reminiscent of the relationship that originally punctuated the notes and pauses of our subjective time. However to think about the end of our journey de-structures our inner harmony and consequently we prevent these moments from capturing our attention for too long, and return to our daily business.

The author is at pain to fully convey his thought and, with his recourse to a great writer, reminds us of *The death of Ivàn I'lìc*, a character who is overwhelmed by futile and unbounded bitterness in the face of his approaching death. Nothing can comfort Ivan, not even the representation of death as the primordial and compassionate companion with her enveloping arms, who features as the third Parca in the "Theme of the Three Caskets".

Lastly, the loneliness of the dying person, to quote Norbert Elias, an author very much present in the book, gives De Masi the opportunity to discuss psychoanalytic treatment in old age. The author spells out that there is a clear-cut distinction between the experience of mourning and the prospect of facing one's own death, which is akin to the nameless dread characteristic of psychotic states. He draws the conclusion that, when addressing the theme of death, it is not at all possible to mobilise the reparative processes which are an integral part of the psychoanalytic treatment, because they are predicated upon the thought of time future, which death negates. Therefore having no other ways of ameliorating this very harsh human predicament, the treatment can only attempt to make it more tolerable or thinkable.

Possibly, the only consoling thought resides in our awareness of a shared, human identity. Thus, feeling close to our fellow human beings allows us to die with the certainty that the world where we have lived and which we have loved will continue to exist and the next generation will go on inhabiting and observing it. De Masi suggests that, in the last analysis, reparation can only occur within a collective context, as it offers us a wider temporal dimension. In this collective time, we work through and transcend our personal finiteness, to merge with other people's sense of time future.

This book is more than a learning experience, as it really opens up a space for personal reflection. I truly believe that those who have the fortune to read it, will close the last page in a pensive silence and with heartfelt gratitude to its author.

INTRODUCTION

Death is not at all a simple presence yet to be realised, it is not at all the ultimate absence reduced to a minimum, but it is, first of all, a looming imminence. Death is the most likely possibility of all our impossibilities.
Martin Heidegger Being and Time

In this book I will endeavour to describe how psychoanalytic theory has explored the theme of the knowledge of death in the individual's unconscious mind, and what inner resources might be available to us to think about this occurrence in the course of our lives and to face it when it is no longer avoidable. I will not, however, examine the philosophical, sociological, religious or mystical approaches to the issue of death, as many scholars have made significant contributions to these.

The awareness of the end of life is always present in us, and it faces us all the time with anxieties, which change in intensity and become more acute when we go through particular moments of crisis. The idea of death does not only concern our biological destiny, but pervades our relationships, all of which are marked by issues of separation and mourning. As a psychoanalyst, I am interested in the quality of the anxiety linked to death as a *natural* occurrence, and consequently I will focus my attention on those aspects that render the thought of death a perturbing one, especially in our western civilisation.

Indeed our culture holds a linear notion of time, according to which individual life, delimited by birth and death, is unique and given only once. From this, it follows that death is considered a final and irrevocable occurrence, clearly opposed to life.

Even though Freud (1920) denied that in the unconscious there might be a representation of one's personal death, he nevertheless speculated on the existence of the death instinct, in other words an unconscious wish to lose oneself in the stillness of death. Freud thought that the progressive disintegration of life through the work of the death instinct occurs silently and without anxiety. According to Freud (1915b), whilst it is difficult to think about one's own death, the death of others can be thought about and represented, painful and disturbing an experience as it may be. We might fear the death of a loved one, anticipate and sense it, even before it happens, and we know we will have to face the emptiness that will ensue.

It is nonetheless difficult to prepare ourselves for the emptiness we will leave. In this case, the word emptiness itself appears to be inaccurate, as we cannot compare it with a sense of fullness. When we ask ourselves how we *understand* death, we are faced with the very limits of our thought.

Every perception, as Husserl pointed out, is endowed with intentionality, the perceptive datum being the product of an activity that captures something from the external world and meets with an object belonging to the realm of shareable experience. Death is not an object on which the subject's intentionality can be founded, because it coincides with the end of all perception. It is a state of things the perceiving subject cannot conceive. We cannot set aside our perceiving function, whilst holding onto it at the same time.

This is why death is located beyond all thinkable experiences.

Yet, if this is how things are, if our own death is unthinkable, what do we mean by "fear of death", what is our representation of death, what is it that torments us?

How can we conceptualise, from a psychoanalytic point of view, the awareness that human beings have of their own death? In what way has death become a concern of psychoanalytic theory?

It is possible to think that psychoanalytic literature, in spite of its thorough exploration of the pain of mourning, has not focused its attention in an equally systematic manner on the bewilderment we feel at the thought of our own death. Harold Searles (1961), an American psychoanalyst, best known for his innovative efforts in the psychoanalytic treatment of psychotic patients, has found it surprising that psychoanalysts have given so little attention to a problem that has a relevant place in every known religion, culture and philosophical system. His conviction is that in every psychoanalytic therapy we should explore the deep meaning the patient attributes to the necessity of death. As psychoanalysts, we should not limit ourselves to exploring issues concerning death in those relatively rare cases of patients, who struggle against serious illnesses, but we should help every patient to develop their capacity to tolerate the thought of the transience of human life. According to Searles, it is precisely the theoretical formulation of psychoanalysis, focused principally on child development, that has prevented us from appropriately thinking about the question of death, and this has occurred independently of the age-old discussions in favour of, or against, a hypothetical death instinct, or of the importance attributed to the symbolic as opposed to the "real" aspects of death.

Perhaps psychoanalysis itself played its part in fostering a certain indifference towards a deeper understanding of our conscious and unconscious ideas about that other face of life, which is death. We should not be overly surprised that we are inclined to forget the thought of our own death all too easily. Although death fantasies are present in every age, the thought of the inevitable end of life tends to remain unexplored until we have gone a long way, at least halfway through the journey of life. Defences against awareness of death have many psychic functions. It is not always easy to clarify how far they facilitate the capacity to live, and how far they may deaden us to the value and meaning of life. On the one hand freedom from the thought of death is often necessary. How could we enjoy success, love, the birth of a child, the pursuit of ideals, without freeing ourselves, at least temporarily, of the notion of death? If death were always present, the awareness of human finite nature would lead to a passive and melancholic acceptance of one's fate and, ultimately, to a destructive view of life.

On the other hand, however, it is not helpful to erase completely the idea of human transience: is it not this, paradoxically, that gives meaning to life? Although death provokes anxiety, it is precisely the thought of the temporal limit of our life that gives meaning to it.

It is only through this awareness that we can stop thinking about life with arrogance and omnipotence.

Without death, we would not be what we are. (2)

This book explores the way psychoanalytic theory has encountered the theme of the transience of human life. To my mind, psychoanalysis has investigated the issue of death from three main points of view. The first concerns the presence or absence of the representation of death in the unconscious; the second links up with the wider theme of separation, loss of objects and loved ones; the third concerns the part played by annihilation anxiety in causing mental suffering. Whilst all three are present in psychoanalytic literature, it is the second, separation anxiety that appears most frequently.

Yet the occurrence of death is not exhausted simply by the pain of the separation from our loved ones; it also carries with it an anxiety about our own disappearance into nothingness, about the dissolution of our own identity and personal history. Whilst in the course of life we can come to terms with our personal losses through the work of mourning, there does not seem to be an equally viable solution when faced with the problem of death. To go through the experience of the ending of our life, we cannot make use of any acquired knowledge, and find ourselves, therefore, in a position of utter loneliness.

As my interest in the theme of death in psychoanalysis originally arose from my clinical experience as a psychoanalyst, the first chapters of the book address death anxiety as it manifests itself in the consulting room. Within the psychoanalytic profession, one cannot avoid confronting daily the problem of death. I am not simply referring here to the experience of inner deadness or the wish to die with which some depressed patients torture themselves and their analysts, but I am also thinking of those who are anguished by death in a dramatic way, experiencing it, as if it were a reality, in their bodies.

During a panic attack, is it not the terrified body that speaks of its own death? Conversely, there are times when an appropriate anxiety seems to be missing. This occurrence is less well known but its consequences are just as complex, as what is missing are the anxiety and pain, which protect us from the risk of dying.

When we are confronted with patients suffering from such very serious psychopathologies as anorexia, drug addiction or psychosis, we can see that they pursue their physical and psychic annihilation without being aware of it or even in a triumphant state of mind. These patients' personalities seem to be dominated by a self-destructive force, which assumes idealised, exciting and positive features.

In this book, I will try to understand why death anxiety might be inevitable. Naturally the cases of serious psychic suffering deserve special attention. To develop my argument, I draw on the psychoanalytic thoughts of Winnicott and the neuroscientific ideas of Edelman, because I think they both offer some useful elements to understand the nature of the pain linked to the dissolution of self and to the lack of future that death represents. In fact, the notion of a potentially infinite development is a constitutional characteristic of our self, an ingrained life-long illusion.

A subjective self, devoid of the notion of development in time, is inconceivable.

Through Winnicott's contribution, we can understand why this belief, an essential constituent of our core self, is thrown into question by the inevitable realisation of our temporal finiteness. Edelman's work helps us understand the reasons why the fear of death acquires a particular intensity in human beings.

We, more than any other living creatures, have developed an historical and affective memory of our own individual experience. This ineliminable conflict between the psychological illusion of infinite development and the necessarily transient nature of our biological structure is at the root of the anxiety and existential crises we go through in the course of our lives. For this reason it seems important to give space to one of the most common of these crises, the mid-life crisis. It is indeed at this time that the hopes, which have contributed to push our individual lives along, might fade, and thus new constructive elements may be needed to renew meaningfulness to the second half of life. I try to describe how this crisis manifests itself, and how, at times, it brings people to look for help with their suffering.

The principal hypothesis of this work is that death, as a natural occurrence, is inscribed in our internal world as a psychotic disaster, a state of disintegration of one's personal identity which is not easy to conceptualise or tolerate.

The representation of death evokes that same nameless dread which overwhelms the psychotic at the time of loss of psychic integration.

I suggest that psychic work is required, throughout life to make this catastrophic occurrence thinkable, and I wonder what emotional resources might be necessary to limit and contain the feeling of loneliness and the pain of death.

My ideas are inevitably sketchy and somewhat provisional. They are a development of what I consider to be the most valuable psychoanalytic theories. These thoughts are meant as an invitation to others, and in the hope that it might be possible through the sharing of ideas to free ourselves partially from the mystery and pain of solitude vis-à-vis death.

In the second part of the book I draw the reader's attention to two very different interpretations of the death instinct, as presented by Sigmund Freud and Melanie Klein.

Placed at the end of the book, this synthesis of the two authors' theories provides a frame of reference for my own thoughts. I recapitulate these sometimes clashing, sometimes complementary theoretical positions, because without them it is impossible to understand the developments and the changes that have taken place in psychoanalytic theory and technique.

The split between Freud and Melanie Klein regarding death anxiety goes beyond a simple contrast, and needs to be seen within the context of their different clinical theories and their conceptualisations of the states of mental suffering.

According to Freud, in fact, mental suffering largely derives from the sacrifice imposed by society (and by the super-ego) to the libidinal instincts, whereas, according to Klein, pain, separation and mourning are linked to the human condition and to the state of primary impotence, which characterises it.

Within the framework of Freud's libido theory, there is no place for death in the unconscious. By contrast, death does have a place in the clinical theory of anxiety put forward by Klein.

NOTES

(1) This is not so in other cultures. In religious India, for instance, a notion of time as cyclical prevails: infinite cycles follow one another, without beginning or ending, marking birth, development, decay and dissolution of whole worlds, which go on existing, embodied in innumerable living beings. Within this perspective, death is not a unique and irrevocable occur-

rence, rather it is just one of the many phases punctuating the uninterrupted rhythm of the transformative life cycle. Thus death is nothing but a pause between lives. (Bergonzi, 2001)

If it is true that a different notion of time makes it possible not to experience death as a brutal caesura of life, it is nevertheless true that in the imagination of the average western person, steeped in a linear concept of life and in the value of the individual, the thought of death is a perturbing element par excellence.

(2) This statement, apparently obvious, but not so obvious psychologically, is pleasantly illustrated by one of Isaac Asimov's stories, *The Positronic Man* (1992). In this story a robot, on discovering his capacity for self-awareness and sensitivity, decides to become a man. Thus he attempts to transform his metallic structure into something similar to the human constitution. However this operation, though technically viable, does not enable him to fit in with other people or make him acceptable, as his virtually immortal positronic brain views him as inhuman, by definition.

PART ONE

Unthinkable Death

1

ON TRANSIENCE

Life is worth nothing, but nothing is worth a life.
André Malraux

Life flies and does not stop an hour
And death follows great days
And things present and past
Are at war with me, and things future too.
Francesco Petrarca

"On Transience" (the German title is *Verganglichkeit*) is a short paper written by Freud in November 1915 for a commemorative book edited by the Berlin Goethe Association.

In this paper, Freud talks about a walk in the mountains, on a really beautiful day, in the company of a young and famous poet (later thought to have been Rilke). (1)

The poet admires the beauty of nature, yet he does not derive any pleasure from it; as he is perturbed by the thought that all that beauty is doomed to disappear.

Reflecting on his young companion's sadness, Freud concludes that a difficulty in tolerating the transience of things can only have two possible outcomes: one is the melancholia affecting the poet, which prevents him from enjoying beauty, the other leads to a state of endless revolt and dissatisfaction.

Beauty, claims Freud, should be appreciated for what it is, even though it may not last. Actually beauty that may not outlast us should be felt as even more valuable. If a flower blossoms just for one night, this increases its charm even more. If beauty is not necessarily long lasting, why is the poet then led to devalue it?

Freud maintains that an inability to enjoy and appreciate the transience of beauty is due to an inability to mourn. The thought of transience puts the poet in touch with the pain of loss and interferes with his capacity to enjoy things. The inability to appreciate beauty comes from a rebellion against temporal boundaries.

Those who cannot mourn, unconsciously reproach their love object for not being perfect, but only finite as humans are. However, there is no love relation without loss; love is always faced by separation. A true capacity to love should entail an appreciation of the object, without the demand that it should always be present or timeless.

These observations acquire a particularly poignant meaning, when we think that Freud was writing them during the First World War, which had destroyed any sense of hope and had spread death and destruction everywhere.

Even during a war it is possible to wonder whether the values that appear to be ephemeral might really lose their meaning forever.

Those who feel too great a despair, perhaps, have not yet worked through their grief. When the war is over and the mourning work done, Freud claims, people will discover that the values of civilization, albeit fragile, are not completely lost.

It will be necessary to rebuild them on a more solid basis and to fight harder to preserve them in the future.

NOTE

(1) Sergio Bordi (1968) has reconstructed the events described in Freud's paper through the letters published by Ernst Freud and Lou Andreas Salomé's diary. In reality Salomé and Rainer Maria Rilke paid a brief courtesy visit to Freud, and had a short evening conversation with him in the hotel drawing room. There was no walk in the beautiful flower-strewn valleys! According to Bordi, Freud's essay in fact reconstructs the emotional exchange between the two men, transposing it in a highly condensed and effective narrative form. During a later meeting, instigated by Lou Andreas Salomé, whose advice the poet sought for a depressive crisis, Freud sug-

gested they go on meeting, but he encountered the poet's net refusal. In a letter to Lou Salomé, Freud expresses his regret that "this highly talented man lets his fear of loss have the better of him". Bordi suggests that the paper "On Transience" might be seen as a successful artistic creation through which Freud elaborated the pain for his failed attempt to help the unhappy poet. "On Transience", together with two other papers, earned Freud the Goethe prize for literature in 1930.

2

THE DENIAL OF TIME AND THE MYTH OF IMMORTALITY

Time is the substance I am made of (. . .) Time is a river that carries me away, but I am that river; it is a tiger that tears me to pieces, but I am that tiger; it is a fire that devours me, but I am that fire.

Jorge Luis Borges

Tomorrow time will disappear with its flashing wings once again, just like yesterday and today. Until I myself will escape the law of time, with my own loftier and shining wings.
From "Singing Over Water", Lieder by Franz Shubert, op. 41, N 2

In a well-known Oriental tale, a high-ranking dignitary meets Death while walking through the city of Isfahan at sunset. At the very moment he recognizes her, he realizes that Death is looking at him with surprise. In a state of terror, he requests an audience from the king and, with his permission to leave the court, he gallops night and day, until he reaches the city of Peshwar, where he thinks he is safe, at last.

The day after, however, at the market, the dignitary runs into Death once again, but this time he realizes he can no longer escape. Before his final surrender, he recalls the surprise they both experienced on their first encounter and brings himself to ask: "Why were you surprised when we met at Isfahan?" and Death replies "I had been told I would meet you at Peshwar, not at Isfahan!"

I quote this story because it well emphasizes, I think, the inevitability of death and the fact that we can only know about it in retrospect, when our life has already come to an end: *mors certa, hora incerta*.

Racing ahead in the attempt to exert some control over the length of his life, the dignitary tries to expand his finite time, so as to postpone the unavoidable time of his own death.

Life moves on all the time, containing the ambiguity of the time of death.

Jankélévitch (1994) states that to have knowledge of one's own death, as those under death sentence do, is a dreadful experience. Not only is death a certainty, as it is for every human being, but the time of death is also certain, which usually is not.

Being certain about both, then life becomes unliveable, because human beings are not made to know the date of their own death, but to remain in a state of uncertainty. (1)

Life is closed by death, but it is always open to hope, which may be experienced as a denial of the necessary occurrence of death.

In Aeschylus' tragedy, Prometheus is a hero who has helped human kind. He is praiseworthy not for his theft of fire from the Gods, but because he obtained from them that human beings be allowed not to know the time of their own death.

Prometheus' gift consists in allowing humanity to live a life without a pre-established limit. But what can the consequences of such ignorance be?

Recalling Countess Dubarry's sorrowful exclamation, in front of the gallows: "One last little minute, Mr. Hangman!" Jean Amery points out that this sentence could well be the expression of the same mistake we make when we think that a suspension of the death sentence is the same as its cancellation.

Aware that we cannot know the time of our own death, we behave as if life should last forever. Even though every living being bears the stamp of temporariness, (time and being coincide), we go about life constantly erasing our awareness of time.

People deal with their awareness of the ending of their own life in the same way as they disavow the question of the inevitable disappearance of life on earth or the possible destruction of our planet: the problem will not concern them, as long as this catastrophe does not become a reality.

In the early years of our childhood, we live happily in the belief that time is infinite. A reasonably secure and protected child goes through infancy discovering the world, with its infinite sensations and pleasures, which s/he encounters every day. The child cannot get his/her mind around the idea that life could be lost forever.

Then, suddenly, the death of a relative, a visit to the graveyard with our mother, a fairy tale, something watched on television puts into our minds, like a sudden and foreign thought, the idea that life might have an ending. Gradually we come to accept the existence of something we call death, which takes away, forever, people we know. (2)

As we become aware of death, we begin to plant in our minds the seeds of the notion of transience.

As human beings, not only do we know when we do not know, but also when we do know something, and we cannot *dismiss* such knowledge. If such knowledge cannot be completely destroyed, still it can go *unnoticed* for a long time. (3)

The kind of awareness of death we acquire is rather peculiar.

Rather than an awareness of our own death, it is an awareness of other people's death. We know that our loved ones might die and therefore we are afraid of being left alone.

On a certain level, we do understand that death concerns everyone, yet deep in our hearts, we go on thinking that it only concerns others. The young think that it is an issue that concerns the old, and not themselves.

The idea of the immortality of the soul pervades both the individual and the collective imaginary. The very notion of immortality comes from the awareness of our mortality. Without one, there would not be the other.

Ethnological studies have shown that every human society creates funeral rituals for their dead, believed to survive or even to be reborn.

Thus, as Morin (1970) notices, death seems to be a kind of life, which extends, somehow or other, the individual's life. This sort of immortality implies an acknowledgement, rather than ignorance of death. Immortality does not come from a disavowal of biology but from its acceptance. The individual can outlast death not so much by working against, but by working with it and accepting it. There are scholars who think that a feeling of immortality is primary in the history of our civilization.

According to Scheler (1984), there have been times in history when the notion of life after death and immortality was an unquestionable assumption. The Hindus, for instance, before the Buddha's preaching, believed in an everlasting life after death, conceived as an endless journey of the soul, in their continual rebirth through the reincarnation cycle.

Paradoxically, Buddha's revolutionary innovation consisted in the claim that the journey of the soul comes to an end, as each of them eventually finds peace in Nirvana. (4) The Judaeo-Christian tradition also locates life beyond its temporal boundary. God has not created Death, which has entered man's life because of original sin. Therefore it is regarded as an unnatural plight.

Some authors think that the current fading of discussions about immortality does not stem from a renewed awareness of the limits of one's personal existence, but rather from a different relationship with death.

One could argue that in these modern times, we are less preoccupied with the issue of immortality, as we no longer live "in the presence of death". Consequently our curiosity about and preoccupation with life after death have decreased.

Gadamer (1993) suggests that the myths deriving from the technological developments of our time have contributed to a sense of omnipotence that allows us to ignore the chancy and uncertain position we have, as inhabitants of this Earth.

The technological rationalism characteristic of our era locates death within its rational circuit, thus removing it from the realm of emotional experience and collective grief.

Our natural tendency to deny death would thus be strengthened by the technological schematism of our times. Our contemporary world has placed death within a scientific form of knowledge, entrusted to the professional skills of those experts who put it within a framework of knowable events and submit it to scientific practices based on measurable efficacy and efficiency.

The organisation of contemporary life (which, effectively does not allow a lot of space and time for pain and grief) in itself would seem to work towards an inhibition of the psychological processes of mourning (Barale, 1982). Our world would thus strive to bring the repression of death, rooted in life itself, to an institutionalised perfection, pushing the notion of transience to the margins of our collective awareness.

At present death is apparently more visible than in the past, having gained utmost screen visibility and also shallowness. Everyday, in fact, the media inform us about death and the cruelty that goes with it: the news is replete with items concerning individual or collective deaths, murders or destruction carried out in every part of the world.

What seems to have been lost is not so much an objective picture of death so much as an emotional awareness and a possibility of working it through.

Marco Guzzi (2001) maintains that ours is probably the first culture that endeavours to provide an answer to the question of death, yet, in reality, it seems to be nothing but an attempt to erase and repress the question itself.

It looks as if our civilisation might simply try to disavow the reality and mystery of death.

NOTES

(1) This is why the possibility of "knowing" our DNA, thus predicting the illnesses inscribed in our genome, turns this knowledge into a bioethical problem.

(2) The child seems unable to conceptualise consciously the idea of death before the age of three or four. It is only around the age of nine or ten that the concept of the end of life becomes a stable intellectual acquisition (Becker, 1973).

(3) Knowledge has, in a certain sense, an olfactory rather than auditory or visual character. Smells, just like knowledge, cannot be wiped out, but only rendered *unnoticeable* if one covers them up with even stronger smells (Bauman, 1992).

(4) Hinduism views life as a series of multiple rebirths (*samara*) which occur within certain conditions resulting from the value of one's accomplishments (*kharma*) .Through good deeds, concordant with one's "task" and role assigned by the caste (*dharma)* it is possible to be delivered from the rebirth cycle (*moksha*) and reach Nirvana.

3

PANIC ATTACK OR IMAGINARY DEATH

Pompa mortis magis terret quam mors ipsa.
(The pomp of death is more frightening than death itself.)
                                                                Francis Bacon

When talking about death anxiety, it is important to distinguish dread from panic.

Fear of future events that threaten our safety can turn into dread, but this does not prevent us from trying to anticipate what we are about to face and also anticipate what our reaction might be. In other words, we can prepare.

Panic, on the contrary, is a sudden reaction of paralysing terror, which belongs to the alarm system of the primitive circuit of fear. Being activated in such an instinctive and automatic way, a panic attack does not permit any planning of an appropriate rational action, fit to deal with the danger, therefore it eludes any possibility to control it. Dread might be equally intense, but its increase is progressive.

Although we must differentiate terror and panic, on the basis of temporal criteria and predictability of the traumatic event, it is nonetheless essential to explore the subjective factors contributing to a state of panic. It is a useful distinction to see terror as deriving from an external danger (reality based fear), whilst panic, on the contrary, could be created by one's imagination. In the latter case, the state of terror is first of all internal, and later projected onto an object, which in itself might well be harmless. Naturally the danger is subjectively real for the person who experiences it.

Similarly, when it comes to death, it is necessary to distinguish fear of death, a feeling common to all human beings, from panic, which, instead, torments only some of us.

There are many people, in fact, who, in the course of their lives, often suffer in dramatic ways for what they experience as their own death. I am talking about panic attacks, which manifest themselves as *somatic* forms of death anxiety. (1)

The person who suffers a panic attack is convinced that his/her own death is imminent. The more acute the somatic symptoms (tachycardia, muscular contractions, abdominal pains, diffused or localized aches, choking, vertigo and excessive perspiration) or the psychological ones (intense and overwhelming anxiety) are, the more unshakable the certainty of an imminent death becomes. It is as if anxiety, held in check for a long time, could spill over, totally uncontained.

During a panic attack, it is the body that speaks of its own death, or rather of its own agony. The psychosomatic symptoms are in the foreground; the mind registers and translates them into unequivocal signs of an unavoidable catastrophe. For example, a light tachycardia can be regarded as a definite forewarning of a heart disease, the sign of an imminent cardio-vascular crisis or, even worse, of a heart attack. The psychic decoding of the event as a catastrophe increases the anxiety, which, in turn, strengthens the somatic signals from which it originates.

Anxiety accelerates breathing, increases heart rate and perspiration, so that very quickly the panic state takes over. The mind is overwhelmed and floods the body, making fear spiral and thus conferring the panic attack that typical characteristic of an imminent dramatic death.

Having occurred once, the panic attack becomes repetitive. After the panic states have subsided, the sufferers are not at all reassured by their survival and by the unfounded nature of their fears; on the contrary, they are ever more inclined to take them seriously. Paradoxically, their survival strengthens their state of alert.

In panic attack sufferers, the neurovegetative circuits, which connect consciousness to danger signals, appear to be so excited, as to have become independent from all rational control. Somewhere in their mind patients "know" they are not going to die, but at the same time they loses their capacity to contain their fear.

Very quickly, a vicious circle gets established, as a consequence of which an automatic response to every signal coming from the body occurs, the attacks tend to repeat themselves and to increase in intensity, even though the contents of the fears are never confirmed. One of the reasons underlying the repetition and the worsening of panic attacks is the connection that memory establishes between stimulus and emotional response. The panic attack, created by the imagination but experienced concretely, is transformed into a *traumatic memory*. Someone who has suffered a great trauma (a railway disaster, for example) will be overwhelmed by anxiety whenever s/he is in a similar situation or in conditions associated with it. Similarly patients suffering from panic states experience intense anxiety whenever their mind reconstructs the mental configuration, which provoked the panic in the first place. Anxiety steadily increases and expands, thus progressively limiting the patient's autonomy. (2) Clearly the mere thought and memory of the panic attack work as trigger. Imagination, with its great magnifying capacity, turns the "traumatic" areas into triggering factors.

Even though its onset may appear sudden, the attack has a slow build up. In a case of somatic panic, the patient begins to listen to his/her body in the same manner in which an earthquake victim pricks up his/her ears for every suspicious noise, every creaking sound of walls and doors in the flat. The patient isolates some suspicious signal up to the point when, in a crescendo of anxiety, s/he can construct, in fantasy, the panic triggering danger. During the panic attack, death is experienced concretely, as the unequivocal sensation of being about to expire. Such a signal, not being associated to a known image or experience, becomes an enigmatic and terrifying event. It is the terrified body that speaks of its own death.

To be able to come out of the panic state, the patient needs an interlocutor who acts as a container of his/her anxiety: in case s/he is alone, it is essential to have a telephone within reach. His/her fear needs to be taken in by a calm and receptive listener.

It is as if a very young child suddenly woke up from his/her sleep, terrified by something painful and threatening: if mother smiles calmly, the new and alarming element will lose its perturbing characteristic.

The panic sufferer is just like a young child, staring at mother's face to try to understand how dangerous whatever has roused his/her attention and threatened the body might really be. If the listener is detached, irritated, or trivialises the catastrophic event, the sufferer's fear will increase to the point of turning into a "nameless dread".

On the other hand, even the slightest emotional resonance, anxiety or doubt can come across as suspicion and confirmation of the possible somatic nature of the illness, thus making the anxiety even more concrete. (3) In this sense, the panic attack makes use of basic and primitive mechanisms, which reveal the persistence of mental processes not yet reached by the functions of affect symbolisation. (4) A peculiar problem of the panic attack, which makes it look like a deadly experience, is the absence of the mental function capable of containing anxiety. If the mind contains the anxiety, this can be recognised and treated as such. It is then possible to say: "I am worried or anxious about something". If, on the contrary, the mind fails this task, the anxiety spills over into the body and turns into deadly panic. Then the thought is: "I am not anxious, I am dying!"

The subjective drama of the experience of panic is tantamount to a "nameless dread", which is such because the mind, unable to contain anxiety, pours it into the body.

In other words, what is brought about is the same constellation as the fear of death, where the body is exposed to its imminent dissolution and the somatic self is in a state of fragmentation.

A patient's backache, another patient's diarrhoea, a pericardial pain become unthinkable, and this results in a breakdown of the psychic containing function with a consequent flooding of the body. Consequences of this state are feared heart attack, dried up aorta, cancer, or a sensation of imminent death. (5)

In these cases the ordinary defence mechanisms, which allow us to forget our fear of death, thereby protecting our existence, seem to be particularly fragile and erratic, and this renders their "psychic skin" permeable.

For one of my patients, the panic attack is like a rent in the skin, it is like a healing surgical wound, closed by a fine thread, which breaks and tears the wound open once again. The skin breaks, the boundary between inside and outside is lost and the anxiety spills over into the body.

At times those who suffer from excessive death anxiety and panic attacks have been children precociously perturbed by a fear of death. This is an example.

A twelve-year-old girl who has come into treatment is terrified by war news, which she listens to on the radio or television and refuses to leave the house. She tells me that she is unable to go to school because she is very frightened by the risk of dying when she is alone, on her way to school. Even staying at home does not completely eliminate the anxiety, because thinking that someone could be in the house, with her, intensifies her fear even more.

She builds up in her mind terrifying events, which she sees as possible, for the sheer fact that she thinks about them. For instance, she is terrified that the sun might crush into the earth and all her family die. As soon as this thought comes to mind, within a few minutes, it turns into anxiety and then into dread. Everything seems to be contaminated by her catastrophic doubt. Who tells us, so the patient thinks, that the laws of nature are so infallible? Could there not be a sudden failure? Why can the sun not crush into the Earth? Likewise, might it not happen that the heart or lungs stop working all of a sudden? Thoughts like this and many other of similar nature torment her to a paralysing point.

The girl's anxiety has begun to undermine some basic vital functions like, for instance, eating. She claims that the she could choke by simply swallowing her food; for this reason, as soon as she begins to eat, she freezes, out of fear. Besides, she was at the table, when she experienced her first panic symptoms. It is her siblings, too many (it is a very large family, indeed) that provoke in her the fear of being invaded, similarly to what happens at school, with her peer group.

As we have seen, the fear of death can develop very early. Because of this anxiety, the adolescent cannot grow up, she loses her sense of personal identity and this loss of self is experienced as an intimation of her own death.

I will report, below, the statements of another adolescent girl, who is going through a period of deep depression, unacknowledged by her family. This girl's most severe symptom, at present, is a devastating anorexia.

The patient says:

> I am really anguished at the thought of death, I feel fated to die young. Life is nothing and I feel already old. When I see someone younger than me, I feel like crying, I feel like an old person, tired of life, unable to change anything. Leopardi was right: it is a good fortune to die in adolescence, so there are no regrets for time past. It must be dreadful for an adult to look at photographs or go over happy memories of the past. I do not want to have happy memories and I do not want to remember anything at all. I feel afraid of death, very afraid. To die old, sad, abandoned; I would rather die now!

She goes on to say:

> I dread growing up and getting old. Growing up means becoming bad, bitter and unhappy (. . .) Last night I had a horrible dream from which I woke up very agitated. In the dream I was with my mother and father, in P., and we were going to die. Only if we had managed to fill in some holes, would we have been able to survive. I was terrified and I was digging the soil with my hands, trying to fill in the hole. At some point, as I was digging, I came across some old objects and an old photograph frame and we became very engrossed in looking at them. However we could not really stop and look, there was no time to waste and had to fill in the holes.

This dream is very effective in evoking the anguish felt at the passage of time, which opens up some devastating gaping holes in this adolescent girl's life. It is essential to fill in the holes of time, which draw her nearer to death; there is no time to look at the past (the photograph frame), which could give meaning and continuity to her life.

Growing up is dangerous and reaching adulthood means losing

one's capacity to love; therefore there is nothing left but a nostalgic contemplation of the past. This is why it is not possible to grow up. Childhood thus turns into a nostalgic object, no longer retrievable, nothing but a continuous source of pain.

Finally, consider a male patient's clinical material, where the dread of the finite nature of life appears very clearly. The patient, still relatively young, fears growing older, feeling that he has not lived his life to the full. He fears death and is phobic about travelling, particularly by plane. Lately, he is contending with the necessity to come to terms with his mother's old age, as she is no longer the energetic and strong-willed person he admired. The patient has the following dream:

> I am in a boat, on a very calm lake. I am on a small rowing boat and the lake is also small. It is dusk and there is not enough time to go on a trip. My mother seems unhappy because time is running out and also because we started late. As I row across the lake, I realise that it is even smaller than I thought, the level of the water has become shallow and does not allow the boat to get through.

Some time later, during an illness of his mother, the patient has another dream about death: "many brown bodies, all in a pile, lie in a flowerbed". He associated an image of dogs to the bodies in the flowerbed. Particularly, what comes to his mind is a breed of dogs that are particularly beautiful but very delicate and have a tendency to die prematurely. The patient is very struck by the colour of the dead bodies, a shitty colour.

It is a pile of dead dogs, in the flowerbeds of life. They are beautiful and lively, but also very fragile and there are many, just like the thoughts about death, which crowd his mind.

In the patient's unconscious mind, death is compared to something contemptible, only good for expulsion. Even though the live object is beautiful and valuable (the beautiful dog), when it dies, it is immediately devalued (it is the colour of shit).

The patient firmly believes that all those people who claim that they remember the dead, in reality bury and forget them. The person who dies is very quickly forgotten and turned into shit.

In this dream the patient is identified with a melancholic object, unable to mourn the loss, and thus only capable of plunging into thoughts about death.

From this patient's unconscious contempt for the transience of life and from his fear of being forgotten, we can understand how much he needs to work through his anxiety about separation, abandonment and death in the psychoanalytic process.

NOTES

(1) Whilst hysteria, the most studied illness of the 19th and the first half of the 20th century, has almost disappeared as a psychopathology, panic attack seems to have become the most common psychological disturbance of our times. It would seem that those who experience the most acute death anxiety are those individuals whose early childhood anxieties have not been contained and processed by their primary object (the mother). In a much greater way than in the past, contemporary psychoanalysis values the environmental factors which are introjected in the course of development and become part of the person's character or individual predisposition. To understand a propensity to experiencing excessive anxiety, inadequate, distorted or failed object relationships are deemed more important than instinctual characteristics. Winnicott, for instance, maintains that the anxiety of falling to pieces or a persecutory anxiety derive from a lack of response of the object, who should be able to take in and put right the baby's anxiety. For Bion, as well, death anxiety is a natural and primitive form of communication projected into the mother, so that she contains and returns it to the infant in a more tolerable form. If the mother cannot transform this anxiety, it turns into a "nameless dread". Within this new theoretical framework, overcoming primitive annihilation anxieties is predicated upon the mother's capacity to understand and return them to the baby in a more digestible form, rather than on the violence of the infant's instinctual drives.

(2) A panic attack does not necessarily get worse over time. Sometimes it is limited to very specific situations: fear of the lift, fear of tunnels, of open spaces, of driving... These symptoms can remain isolated and fade or disappear completely within a few months. The onset of the panic attack can occur during the day or at night. In this case, the feeling of being about to die can be made even more terrifying by nocturnal loss of consciousness.

(3) Panic can occur when the individual does not have a mental apparatus for the psychic registration of negative emotions. The psychological stimuli are translated into a body language, which, by definition, cannot be represented mentally. Panic attacks seem devoid of any connection with the subject's emotional or relational life. Freud himself had classified them as

"actual neuroses", differentiating them from psychoneuroses, which could be linked with significant past experiences.

(4) One of the differences between hysteria and panic (or as Freud would say, "conversion hysteria" and "anxiety hysteria") is that the hysterical symptom always results from a symbolisation process, which is missing, instead, in a panic attack. In the latter, it is the imagination that emphasises the annihilation anxiety.

(5) The uncertainty concerning the body's integrity, which is the basic factor in panic attacks, involves a problematic relationship of the body with space, as well. Claustrophobia, as fear of being invaded, or agoraphobia, as fear of disappearing in a vast, open and lonely space, represent a constant threat for people who live with an unstructured sense of self.

4

PSYCHIC STRATEGIES TOWARDS SELF-ANNIHILATION (1)

He wanted to reduce the part of himself exposed to
the world,
And sleep until everything would be over.
                              Albert Camus, *The Happy Death*

He does not lose anything, for with the loss of himself,
he loses the knowledge of loss.
                                      Jack London, *Sea Wolf*

In Jack London's novel *Martin Eden* the main character, after fighting strenuously, succeeds as a writer, but then has to face the most severe crisis of his life.

At this point, he discovers that the values, such as friendship and love, in which he has always believed, are systematically dismissed by the hypocritical world surrounding him.

His admirers and the woman he loved, who did not show him any sympathy when he was lonely and suffering, now recognise him as a successful man.

The sudden collapse of his illusions drives Martin Eden to drown himself.

Martin is not afraid of death. He has faced death many times in his life; maybe he has sought it, and has never been afraid of it.

After letting himself slide through a porthole of the ship he is travelling on, he then starts instinctively to swim as though he wanted to reach the distant shore.

Only after a short while, his suicidal intent comes back to his mind.

> ... it was the automatic instinct to live. He ceased swimming, but the moment he felt the water rising above his mouth, the hands struck out sharply with a lifting movement. The will to live, was his thought, and the thought was accompanied by a sneer.

In the end, he has enough will power to be able to go under water, in a last successful effort to put an end to his existence.

> He breathed in the water deeply, deliberately, after the manner of a man taking an anaesthetic. When he strangled, quite involuntarily, his arms and legs clawed the water and drove him up to the surface and into the clear sight of the stars. The will to live, he thought disdainfully, vainly endeavouring not to bring the air into his bursting lungs.

Only at the end does Martin decide to throw himself into the abyss, swimming wildly towards the bottom of the sea, until he has no oxygen left, so as to preclude himself from any possible re-surfacing.

I have quoted this passage from Jack London's novel to emphasise the strength of our survival instinct.

This will, inscribed in our biological constitution, strenuously opposes any movement in the opposite direction.

The will to survive is shown by the instinct, which drives Martin to save himself, each time, despite his unequivocal suicidal intention.

The fear of dying is ineliminable and is with us all our life; it is a danger signal, whose function is to protect us from possible threats.

When it is not excessive or felt to be a persecution, the anxiety we feel in the face of death is a sign that we have retained, in our inner world, those self-preservative drives which give value to life and protect it. In other words, death anxiety is an alarm signal, whose function can be to communicate a need for help.

In the previous chapter I recalled that we psychoanalysts are used to dealing with the very intense death anxiety experienced by patients suffering from panic attacks.

Death anxiety, however, is not always and not only a symptom of psychopathology.

There is also another instance, not so well known or emphasised in psychoanalytic writings, characterised by the absence of the usual defences which protect us from pain, suffering and death. The more severe the psychopathological conditions, the more remarkably absent the anxiety in relation to one's own physical, psychic and emotional death. It is this very absence that, in the face of a clear self-destructive behaviour, causes a silent and inescapable sliding towards death

The nature of this silent movement must be put at the centre of our investigation. In this way we can better understand how it might operate in certain forms of mental suffering and identify its special and traumatic underlying aetiology.

We have yet to explore how the self-destructive drive, by losing its emotional connection with signal anxiety and pain, turns into the pleasure of self-annihilation.

The risk of accomplishing one's own physical or psychic death is a rather frequent occurrence in cases of serious mental pathology.

This can be seen, for instance, in severe melancholia, where hatred towards life and the Ego, with its wish to live, is so intense that Freud talked about the melancholic Super-Ego as a pure culture of the death instinct. The impulse towards suicide is the immanent condition of the melancholic state and is fuelled by the power of the Super -Ego, which blames the patient for failure and demands the ultimate sacrifice.

We must note, however, that even though death wishes can be linked to delusional guilty feelings, the melancholic is always aware of aiming towards death and doesn't deny it.

In other mental conditions, which also drive towards death, the situation is very different In anorexia nervosa, for instance, the patient is not aware of being ill or in pain, and denies that the anorectic behaviour can lead to death.

Indeed, food refusal is not felt to be an abnormal behaviour, rather it is turned into an extraordinary experience: because of her omnipotence, the anorectic is not aware that her attraction towards this mental state is the equivalent of an attraction towards death.

In many cases the drive towards death acts secretly and quietly; these patients' personalities seem dominated by a self-destructive force, which presents itself with idealised, exciting and positive features.

Mental areas charged with self-destructive impulses are formed: these are silent psychotic islands, which remain within the personality, ready to break out at times of crisis. In less severely ill patients, those we meet more frequently in our psychoanalytic work, the attraction towards death might appear in dream images of beautiful landscapes in which a cemetery appears particularly pretty or is painted in lively colours. One of my patients, traumatised in her childhood, in a particularly sad and difficult period in her life as well as in her analysis, dreamt of flying over a little town, located on a cliff dropping sheer to the blue sea, a very beautiful Mediterranean landscape, and wishing to dive into that sea. The patient associated the little town over the sea with the Greek island where her father, together with other Italian officers, had been shot by German soldiers and thrown into the sea.

A characteristic feature of these mental states and these dreams is their lack of anxiety, which, together with an idealisation of death, allows self-destruction to be acted out. One of the first works in which the subject of attraction towards death has been explored, within a psychoanalytical perspective, is surely Karl Abraham's "Giovanni Segantini: a Psychoanalytical Essay" (1911). Segantini has a very difficult childhood. Already at the age of five he is an orphan, moved from the care of relatives to community homes. When he becomes a successful artist, his creativity seems nourished by his love for his mother, who had died prematurely. Some of his best works are, in fact, representations of mothers absorbed in their own thoughts. Segantini becomes extremely sensitive to the problem of death, loss and grief. Sadness and melancholic grief inspire the paintings of his late maturity and his latest mystical-fantastic works; piety and love are replaced by a sense of desolation and death. Escape from reality and fascination with self-annihilation seem to be his latest passions.

Effectively, death triumphs in the end; determined as he was to be by himself in the mountains to paint, Segantini falls ill, refuses medical help and eventually he is found dying in front of his palette.

Death seems to have been born with him and never to have abandoned him, in spite of his attempts to deny, contain or transform it.

Abraham compares two of Segantini's dreams on the subject of death; the first one, an anxiety-ridden dream from a few years previously, and the last one, in which the artist sees his own painting (on the theme of death) leaving his mountain house in a coffin before his wife who watches in tears.

Segentini himself had reported this dream to his wife, before he got to the mountains.

According to Abraham, in the first dream the anxiety comes from his wish to live, whilst in the latter his submission to and fascination with the approaching death prevail.

In *Beyond the Pleasure Principle* (1920) Freud presented the death instinct as an unstoppable biological force silently at work in every living being.

As has repeatedly been observed, Freud's views appear to be founded on a psychologically deterministic assumption, since he equates biological death to the destructive forces at work within the mind.

The importance of the death instinct in psychic life was later formulated by Melanie Klein and her followers, who understood that some psychopathological states, whose treatment presents noticeable difficulties, are sustained by a destructive mental organisation that attacks the healthy parts of the personality.

This type of approach, however, does not clarify the aetiological factors, which could predispose those people who will become prospective patients to develop, in childhood, the self-destructive passion, ultimately leading to their self-annihilation.

In contemporary psychoanalytic literature there are a number of hypotheses, which do not consider destructiveness (directed against the self or against others) as innate or instinctual, but rather as created and strengthened by environmental pressures of a traumatic nature.

These new notions of psychic trauma can help us understand how a child, prematurely exposed to very unfavourable circumstances, could internalise a particular tendency to destroy his life instinct.

Denial of needs and self-annihilation may be a response to a prolonged traumatic exposure, when the child is still very small and dependent and his anxieties are too intense to allow alternative and more adaptive defences.

A persistent lack of maternal empathy may be traumatic.

According to Winnicott (1971), a baby's ability to experience its presence in the world as significant, results from a good relationship with a mother who permits and tolerates the experience of a blissful union. When this need is systematically threatened or attacked, the wish to live and the sense of going on being are disturbed and an attraction towards a state of not being ensues.

Rosenfeld (1978) has investigated these psychopathological states, identifying some characteristics of borderline patients in relation to their traumatic experiences. He believes that the prolonged suffering a small child experiences when its annihilation anxiety is not met by an empathic maternal response, forms an early core of potential self-destructiveness. In these cases, according to Rosenfeld, the systematic attack to the libidinal self, as an attempt to silence the experience of intolerable suffering, would be a possible response to the trauma.

Anger and hatred, initially directed against the mother, because of her failed affective response, are then directed against the libidinal self, held to be responsible for the unbearable suffering and attacked mercilessly.

Both Winnicott and Rosenfeld emphasise that early and repeated traumas, such as a systematic disavowal of the child's needs, are like a time bomb, bound to explode later on.

Anger and rejection of life obliterate any survival instinct and lead certain individuals to pursue and idealise death in a triumphant state of mind. When the life instinct is absent, death anxiety does not develop.

The drive towards self-annihilation thus represents an unconscious, dramatic and paradoxical response to trauma and early intolerable pain, reactivated in the course of life.

In some cases, a disruption of the ego's capacity to feel anxiety is accompanied by states of lethargy, numbness, obtuseness, anaesthesia or voluptuous and ecstatic pleasure.

I think these mental conditions call for some observations on the nature of the pleasure, which sustains the self-destructive movement.

To illustrate this point, I would like to present two clinical accounts.

The first concerns a 35 years old patient, with a non-cohesive self. His academic life and later his work life seemed to have come to a standstill. In the analysis, the patient usually expresses himself in a bizarre and enigmatic way.

During a session, he tells me how, in his youth, he felt as if he was "flowing away" and how he watched, helplessly and passively, his failure, thus dissipating his own self and his youth. In the first phase of the analysis, the patient wishes to become a tramp, so as to be able to lose himself completely.

He remembers reading and quotes reports of states of heavenly pleasure experienced by people about to die or drown: the dying person overcomes his death anxiety and his agony turns into enlightenment, peace, and sweet annihilation. The patient now recognises how, in his youth, this self-induced autoerotic pleasure had made him passive and unable to face the awareness of his unstoppable failure and psychological catastrophe.

In this case annihilation and sensual pleasure coincide.

The second case involves a male patient, who has been in analysis for one year, after a number of psychotherapeutic treatments. He sought treatment for his severe symptoms that began with phobias, an eating disorder and death anxiety, and eventually led to his isolation and difficulty in attending school.

At the age of 15, M. had started feeling considerably ill; he could not eat, he was terrified by the thought of death, he felt locked in a dead object, a coffin, and unable to scream to signal his terror.

During periods of isolation he felt particularly compelled to watch porno videos, which gave him long spells of exciting pleasure.

Upon seeing him for the first time, he appeared very ill. He has been house-bound for months and has made a tremendous effort to reach my consulting room, because, as soon as he leaves home, he fears getting lost, being squashed or laughed at.

He reports having gone through a spell of insomnia, now over. In the morning, however, he cannot get out of bed; he holds on to his night dreams because they are the only glimmer of life he has left, his only reality.

During the day he does not feel alive, he stays in bed waiting for his parents to come back from work.

In the last few months it is as though he has regressed; he literally feels a very small baby, or even a foetus.

Before he came into analysis, he had had the illusion of being very important; he was certain that he was in telepathic contact with the television whose characters winked and smiled at him.

Now he has such a profound need to sink into an object, that he really struggles to get up from the chair or the analytic couch, when he uses it. He feels his muscles to be heavy and walks with exasperating slowness.

In the first few weeks of therapy, we are in the presence of a heavily binding force that pulls him down, closes him off, and removes him from life and from me. He faces a daily struggle to come to his sessions, especially in the couple of hours leading up to them.

The patient knows that giving into this force would mean to be stifled; on the contrary the struggle he has to keep up to oppose it, makes him feel alive.

At the same time as he gives up his delusional and hallucinatory states (grandiosity, bodily transformation), his anxiety re-emerges, for the painful and intolerable awareness of his losses caused by his incapacity to progress, to form relationships, and his reliance on a masturbatory and pornographic world.

After the first few months of analysis, which appear to be significant and very intense, as well as tense and anxiety-ridden, the patient suddenly changes.

I often find him lying down on the sofa or asleep in the armchair when I fetch him in the waiting room; during the session he is silent, he remains for the whole time in a state of pleasant lethargy and changes position, only to sleep more comfortably.

If he talks, it is only to express his satisfaction with the food eaten in solitude. If he could, he tells me, he would visit prostitutes every day. He does not understand why other people do not sleep like him, why they give up a world of total pleasure.

When I tell him that he fills himself with hypnotic pleasure and wipes out my presence, as though he could completely disregard myself and everybody else, he replies that he considers me too optimistic with regard to life and too pessimistic with regard to death.

To clarify, he adds that he worries because he is only 24. He would like to have lived more of his life; then he would be closer to the "second life". The trouble is, he comments, that since starting his analysis, he has begun to doubt the existence of this "second life".

This "second life" fascinates him; it has an almost hypnotic power over him.

It is a deadly force disguised as pleasure, a voluptuous and lethargic state in which he can immerse himself. In the early phase of his analysis, he felt anxious and alive, very worried about the thought of time past and lost, now he immerses himself in a timeless, anxiety-free and pleasurable lethargy.

Freud sets pleasure against reality. In "Formulations on The Two Principles of Mental Functioning"(1911), he suggests that the pleasure principle precedes the reality principle and continues to be active even after the latter has established itself. The sexual drive, fantasy and dream, being mental activities with the ability to reproduce themselves, are expressions of the pleasure principle removed from the reality principle, and become a parallel mode of mental functioning.

The stage of life when pleasure prevails, according to Freud, is a primitive nucleus of life.

This hypothesis greatly influenced early psychoanalytical theories about pleasurable mental states. As these states are considered to be archaic, they are regarded as accessible only through regression.

Alexander (1951), for instance, in his description of states of well-being and bliss, obtained through Buddhist meditation techniques (see Epstein, 1990), points out that, in meditation, one is totally absorbed in a pleasurable state, which he calls narcissism and, in agreement with Freud, he regards as a regression to a primitive pre-object phase.

Janine Chasseguet-Smirgel (1986) explores further this backward movement in her description of perverse or borderline patients. She suggests that they experience an uncontrollable drive towards total gratification, an illusory lost paradise, where they do not feel any need or tension and where they are the sole inhabitants of the maternal world. For this author, the desire to return to a womb-like state, eliminating every possible obstacle on the way toward the maternal body, seems to be the same instinct that Freud, in *Beyond the Pleasure Principle,* calls death instinct.

It follows, however, that if the death instinct and pleasure converge, Freud's hypothesis, formulated in 1920, becomes untenable.

Indeed to lay the theoretical foundation of the death instinct, Freud starts from the opposite premise, according to which the death instinct overruns and negates the pleasure principle, thus being closely connected, instead, to displeasure.

The aim of this drive, rather than pleasure, is a search for displeasure. Consequently the recourse to an anti-libidinal or a death drive becomes necessary.

At the Symposium on the death instinct, held in Marseille in 1986 by the European Federation of Psychoanalysis, Hanna Segal stated that primary narcissism is a manifestation of the death instinct.

She also pointed out that intense love for oneself is not the same as narcissism, which is merely an expression of the death instinct in its de-objectalising function (according to Green's felicitous definition, 1986). In other words, the essence of narcissism consists in severing any link with the object.

If we conceptualise narcissism as closely linked to the death instinct, we must ask ourselves what particular meaning it takes in the patient's experience.

In other words, what attracts patients so irresistibly to distance themselves from the object?

In my view the primary narcissistic condition is hypothetical and unproved. I believe that some individuals have the capacity to bring about a silent change in their minds, through an addictive autoerotism. It is precisely this self-induced pleasure what exerts a pull towards death under the aegis of narcissism and the pleasure principle.

Therefore we witness the emergence of a state of "negative", self-destructive pleasure.

The addictive nature of this pleasure accounts for the patient's passivity when faced with the disaster that silently consumes him.

Freud understands the death instinct in two incompatible ways: on the one hand as a catastrophic occurrence, destructive and self-destructive for the Ego, on the other as a quiet return to the Nirvana state.

It is not so easy to establish whether these two views imply disparate phenomena, or whether they indicate different aspects of the same experience. This ambiguity, or even contradiction, has led many to question the value of this particular work by Freud. Is this passive self-annihilation, this silent return to the foetal state, really so quiet, peaceful, conflict and anxiety-free as patients would like us to believe?

Some authors think that there is an inborn capacity to regress to a quasi-foetal mental state. To this effect, Horton (1974) states with regard to the experience of mysticism:

> Our understanding of primary narcissism and the forms of its transformation makes it clear that the intrauterine mode of relating, characterised by receptivity-passivity, represents an indelible part of the human psyche.

The author points out, however, that the employment of narcissistic defences and the return to primary narcissism must not be confused with psychosis.

Within this framework, then, regression to a foetus-like state represents a transient and reversible phenomenon of return to a primitive condition, rather than the outcome of destruction, albeit apparently silent.

This foetus-like condition, whose foundations are the principles of constancy and inertia, would thus be a protective shield against an excess of stimuli, similar to what Freud regarded as the Nirvana principle.

According to other analysts, however, this regressive mental state, subjectively experienced as being enveloped in a cocoon, is in reality a destructive process, with dramatic consequences and as such it is registered by the unconscious.

In "On the Clinical Usefulness of the Concept of the Death Instinct", Hanna Segal (1993) talks about the deadly panic felt by one of her patients, whose fantasy to return to a foetal state was experienced as a process of violent mutilation of legs, arms and eyes, leading to a transformation into a shapeless embryo. She emphasises that the desire to return to a foetal state is not as idyllic as one might think; rather it is a violent process of self-mutilation involving the need to cut one's sensory organs off.

Rosenfeld (1986) reports the case of a patient who, after telling a dream, had sunk into a motionless silence, interpreted by the analyst as an attempt to avoid any contact with him, because of her wish to remain alone and reject the psychoanalytic work. In the following session, the patient had become unmanageable, in the grip of inexplicable anger.

It was not clear whether the silence of the previous session was a defence against her anger or if her rage was a response to the interpretation, which she felt had forced her to relate to the analyst.

A few weeks later, the patient had revealed withholding from her analyst that in her dream she was totally motionless and contained in the maternal womb. Her silence therefore was not a defence against her anger; rather it represented her desire to recreate, in the session, a foetal state and had responded with rage to feeling forced into being born.

This example shows how hard it is to tell how much contact a patient can tolerate and how difficult it can be to measure our intervention. Indeed, the use of interpretation can induce panic and anger and, consequently, push the patient back into the unbearable state s/he is running away from.

This understanding of anxiety and rage is particularly important, and it helps explain how I provoked angry reactions in the patient who talked about a "second life" and consequently attacked me in response to all my interventions. This occurred during a phase of the analysis when he painfully stated that he had lost his usual recourse to sleeping as a source of pleasure in his sessions.

In fact he has difficulty coming to his sessions, because every perception he has is felt to be an irritant. In the same way as his dog furiously burrows his bed into the carpet, so at the beginning of the session the patient sinks into the couch, turning it into his cocoon. Attempts to help him re-emerge from this mental state led him to violently punch the couch and scream.

When I break his silence with my interpretations, it is as if I am attacking him. If on the one hand the patient, when stimulated to abandon his foetal position, is overwhelmed by anxiety and anger, on the other hand the withdrawal he achieves through his self-hypnotic fascination deprives him ever more of his defensive system.

When he emerges from his lethargy, he feels helpless, exposed, pierced by objects and gripped by terror. The lethargic auto-hypnotic or autoerotic position, meant as a protective shield, in reality destroys his mind.

A female analysand, after several hospital admissions for psychotic episodes, had struggled to re-establish herself in the family and to realise that the hospital was not the centre of the world, the idealised place where she could believe she was an adolescent queen free from responsibilities and anxieties.

Although she has made progress, any contact with life is always very difficult for her.

She stays in bed for hours and is unable to look after her house and feel alive in her relationships with her children. To fight an unbearable sense of emptiness, she must go to bed and withdraw into a state of dreamy pleasure.

In one of her sessions she describes the changes in her room; with her camomile tea, cigarettes and the telephone by her bed, she feels like a Sheik surrounded by his bayaderes, immersed in a world of utter sensual pleasure.

This patient, just like the other, protects herself from pain by putting her mind to sleep and paralysing it; however, through her pleasure, in reality she obliterates and destroys parts of herself and her psychic qualities.

When she comes out of this mental state, she feels anxious and claustrophobic, she cannot orient herself in her daily life and no longer remembers how to start her washing machine. Describing these experiences when a part of her mind is unable to function, she calls them "early dementia" or "psychic stroke", which she associates with alcohol and the psychotropic drugs she persistently uses.

Bègoin (1989) claims that postulating the existence of the death instinct in psychoanalysis is meaningless. According to Bègoin, what we see are not manifestations of the death instinct, but defences against the experience of primitive, unbearable depressive pain. This excessive psychic pain leads to psychotic defences. There is a close and inseparable link between intolerable anxiety and the destruction of one's organs resulting from the fantasy withdrawal into the foetal position.

We need to understand, each time, whether the anxiety comes from an inability to contain mental pain or rather from the consequences of the self-destructive defences and from changes in the perceptive apparatus.

Underlying the foetal regression, there is a murderous hatred of life and mind, in response to intolerable pain. The defensive regression, affecting the perceptive apparatus, aims at distancing the patient from those unbearable emotions.

Therefore pain, hatred and anger are aroused and directed against the analyst whenever s/he comes alive, through making an intervention.

Patients tell us how they are unable to tolerate psychic pain, deprivation, confusion and mental catastrophe. There are mental states in which thinking or even just being awake is painful. To protect themselves, some patients need to cut off their minds and destroy their perceptive apparatus. To them this appears to be the only possible solution.

The mental pain caused by being alive can only be placated by withdrawal into a state of non-being.

With the most severely ill patients, it is particularly important to understand what might be the pain they need to face and what resources might be available to them.

Also, we have to bear in mind that the patient is in a state of precarious psychic equilibrium and is constantly in danger of breaking down.

In the treatment of these cases, a very critical time comes when the patient emerges from his withdrawal and becomes aware of his/her suffering. If this awareness proves to be too painful, a further retreat may seem again the only solution.

When they come to understanding that they have seduced themselves and distorted their sense organs, this insight provokes feelings of guilt for their self-destructive behaviour.

This intolerable guilty feeling can easily induce them to regress, strengthen their self-destructive defences and murder their minds once more, in a desperate attempt to destroy their awareness of their catastrophic past as well as their persecutory anxieties.

By manipulating their perceptive organs and their minds, these patients reproduce a foetal-like state, experienced as pleasurable and blissful.

It is the "happy island" described by the patient who talked about a "second life". During a very meaningful session, in which he had gained some lucid, albeit transient, self-awareness, he then added:

> 'Something very powerful has happened, which has distanced myself from my most straightforward feelings and from my friends; I have left behind what was close, in search of something far away, instead.'

In that session he had been able to clarify that his violent reaction to my efforts to help him out of his lethargy was an expression of his rage for the help he was indeed receiving from me.

He could not tolerate being helped; my assistance, which was good and bad at the same time, prevented him from satisfying his need to remain cocooned in his own body as though it were a "happy island".

Permanence on the "island" was his only source of happiness, even though this entailed being parent-less and "leg-less".

Probably each of us has the potential to bring about psychic death by withdrawing into an ecstatic and autoerotic state.

These mental states, not infrequent in psychological illnesses, have something in common with mystical and ecstatic experiences, which are, in any case, forms of psychic retreat.

In psychopathology, the pleasure attached to self-destruction appears to be linked to an omnipotent fantasy with two complementary aspects: transgressive eroticism and autoerotic withdrawal.

I would like to point out that the body is involved in this process; the patient is enveloped in the body, and in this way becomes the fantasised embryo. Essentially, the containing womb is his/her body.

A mind-body fusion obtains with the aim of obliterating the mind and the Ego, through a process of "de-mentalization".

In the foetal position, the body becomes not only a locus of retreat from the world, but also a vehicle of autoerotic pleasure and perceptive omnipotence.

By foetal position I do not just mean a transient regressive experience as such, but a destructive effort to obliterate and change the perceptive apparatus, which locks the patient into a pleasurable sensory prison.

Like other psychotic changes, this also runs the risk of becoming an irreversible mutilation of the mind.

Regression to a uterine state is not at all an easy or tranquil occurrence. There cannot be a peaceful regression to a Nirvana state, understood as a return to the maternal womb; the foetal position is achieved through the destruction of the psychic apparatus and the emotional and relational reality.

One of the early symptoms of the patient who talked about a "second life" had been the anxiety of being imprisoned in a coffin, cut off and far from any possible help.

The coffin represented the autoerotic retreat we could define as a uterine position, which the patient himself feared to be a place of no return.

Unconsciously the patient knew that his state of foetal retreat, initially accompanied by heavenly and voluptuous pleasure, had later revealed itself to be an agonizing trap, not so easy to leave behind once the signs of the life instinct reappeared.

NOTE

An earlier version of this paper is published with the same title in the *Rivista di Psicoanalisi*, vol. 42, N.4 (1996)

5

FEAR OR SERENITY?

Those who talk about me do not know me and, when they speak,
they slander me; those who know me, keep quiet, and in their silence,
 they do not take my side; thus they all curse me until they meet me,
but when they meet me they rest and go past, even though I never rest.
    Xavier Marìas, *Tomorrow in the battle think about me*

The poor devil who walks up to the gallows with composure,
the great sage who utters aphorisms after he's emptied the cup of hemlock,
the captured freedom fighter who smiles when he sees the rifles aimed at his chest –
they're all just hypocrites. I know that their composure, their smile are all a character.
For they're all terrified of death, hideously afraid because such a fear is as natural as death itself.
                    Arthur Schnitzler, *Dying*

In a paper written in 1988, Emanuele Bonasia suggests that the theory of the death instinct and the interpretation of the annihilation anxiety arising from the former are but an attempt, on the psychoanalysts's part, to reduce the real fear of death to a personal problem. In other words, his hypothesis is that psychoanalysts have a tendency to use theory defensively and are, indeed, unable to provide adequate answers to a real terror.

Psychoanalysis could be used to rationalize and deny the catastrophic impact that the fear of death has on all human beings, including psychoanalysts, through an indirect attempt to pathologize it. Analysts might employ every available means to show their patients how their fears are symptomatic, whilst unconsciously they, themselves, are in the grip of the same anxiety.

In this respect, we can see a curious similarity between the importance that castration anxiety has for Freud and the central part played by persecutory anxiety in Melanie Klein's thought.

Michael Eigen (1996) remarks how Freud seems to think that, if castration anxiety could be resolved, there would not be any pathological fear of death.

Whilst Freud seems to imply that castration anxiety causes the fear of death, Melanie Klein suggests that, if we could adequately work through our persecutory anxieties, we would not be tormented by the terror of dying. Both of them appear to set aside the real anxiety, and think that it may be possible to achieve Socrates' calm posture vis-à-vis death. (1)

Is it really possible to accept fully the "Socratic" implications of Freud and Melanie Klein's theories and view death anxiety as a symptom of a malady of the soul? Socrates' serene posture vis-à-vis death as well as Freud's and Klein's theoretical efforts to trace death anxiety back to something else are not easily compatible with a shared, human experience of an irreducible fear of dying.

Indeed, why should we not experience the threat to our personal self as disquieting? Let us think about the understandable apprehension we experience during a medical examination, whenever we come into contact with warning signals from our bodies, and the inevitable relief we feel, when we realise that it was just a false alarm.

Is it really possible to come to a fearless representation of the destruction of our self in the process of dying? Besides, does this fear not have a useful function? (2)

As a matter of fact, experiencing alarm mobilises our behavioural response (fight or flight), which produces life defences necessary to our self-preservation. These defences are paralysed whenever very intense anxiety turns into panic.

We are endowed with self-protective mechanisms, inscribed in our biological constitution, that are necessary for our survival. These defensive systems signal danger and activate an instinctive response, inborn and instinctive, even before the nature of the threat is ascertained.

Human beings' fear of external danger, experienced through the perceptive channels and necessary to their survival, is not essentially different from the fear other living species feel. If, for instance, we are walking along a dark road or through a wood, we respond with alarm and run away as soon as we become aware of a noise or a shadow. Only afterwards do we try to ascertain whether we felt a real or imaginary threat.

Likewise an animal usually responds to a noise with flight or absolute stillness. Still the same animal, apparently unaware of death, mobilises his defences if aware of a mortal danger linked to something unknown, or associated with attacks or some hostile presence. Therefore the fear of death is an alarm signal whose function is the preservation of life.

These observations lead us to reflect on our psychoanalytic understanding of the problem of the *real fear of our real death*. How can we make death thinkable, when it is both an unthinkable and a disquieting presence in our minds?

Why does the fear of death become excessive only in some specific circumstances of our lives? What psychic resources should we be endowed with, to oppose and contain the anxiety we feel at the awareness of our finite nature?

I cannot help quoting here, albeit briefly, Heidegger, who founds his philosophical research on the fear of death. Some of the German philosopher's ideas concern us closely, as they are similar to what we hear in our consulting rooms and link with my own formulations.

According to Heidegger, the anguish we experience when we are aware of the nothingness of our being is the truth of our being in the world. Our very existence is disturbing for us, as we inhabit a world where we live in order to die. Heidegger maintains that, in the anticipation of death, indeterminate, but certain, our *being there* is exposed to an immanent threat coming from its own presence (*there*).

Death anxiety, which must be differentiated from *fear of dying*, is unavoidable.

To counteract the fear of dying, many philosophers, like Socrates or Epicures, have argued that the question itself is a futile one. Nevertheless understanding that we live only to die is a different experience from the fear of dying. Living itself is actually the same as dying. Understanding this may be disturbing. Heidegger proposes a well-known solution. When we discover the true essence of our being in the world, we should not allow our anguish to overwhelm us, rather we should face the truth and understand that death is the closest possibility to our being alive.

Once our anguish has revealed that we cannot be but nothingness, our awareness of *nothingness* deprives death of its power. In accepting death as our immanent destiny, we achieve a higher level of autonomy. Awareness of death, in fact, confronts us with the possibility of being ourselves, free from illusions. However, this freedom, in its turn, cannot be free of the thought of death, which, on the contrary, should continue to be our necessary companion, placed at the core of our being.

Our being-there can be authentic only if we are able to experience a premonition of our own death; therefore anxiety is the emotion that accompanies our authenticity, because it alerts us to the transient nature of all things.

NOTES

(1) Socrates maintains that the thought of one's death should not cause anxiety: if death is absence of consciousness, akin to a deep dreamless sleep, then it should not be feared. If we all tried to remember a dreamless night and compared it to other more upsetting nights and days, we would realise there are few moments better than the dreamless night that death is. Conversely, if death is the passage from this world to another, where we can find the best people dead before us, then it is even something good. In Fedon, Plato states that death occurs when the mind is delivered from the body, thus mind and spirit are freed, at last, from our bodily prison. In *Lectures in Metaphysics* Kant also states that spiritual life does not cease

when the body dies, and that immortality is the natural necessity of life. When the body ceases to live, the soul frees itself from its obstacle and it really begins to live from then on.

(2) Human beings display an emotional response to death as if it were a trauma. Such response seems to be at variance with most philosophical theories, inspired by Epicures, developed by the Stoics and picked up by the Encyclopaedists and later by Feuerbach (Morin, 1970). According to these philosophers, death corresponds to nothingness. "After death, everything ends, including death itself", states Seneca. Lucretius writes: "Do we not see that when death comes, nobody will be there to suffer the pain of the loss of himself?" These philosophical theories erase the psychic experience of death, wiping out its traumatic aspect.

6

POTENTIAL SELF AND ABSENCE OF FUTURE

Without future, the present is useless,
it is as if it did not exist.
Josè Saramago, *Blindness*

Despair is absence of future. Therefore, insofar as death is absence of future, the destruction of every possible future, whatever it might be or however improbable it might be, death is loss of hope.
Vladimir Jankélévitch *To Think of Death?*

Freud never developed the notion of self. Seemingly, in his writings, he only talks about the Ego, the psychic agency endowed with individuality, body and concreteness and also able to be in contact with the external world. (1) Melanie Klein also did not develop the concept of self, which she uses only in rare occasions (1946) and only descriptively.

Winnicott is the first analyst who puts forwards a developmental model of the self (1958), which he regards as innate potential and as the psychic equivalent of the body, with its ability to grow and develop its functions.

Winnicott's self is what gives the individual the sense of being an autonomous and separate person, different from other selves and this is the product of the maturational process. In the presence of a favourable facilitating human environment, the maturational process fosters the development of the self, formed by various parts joining together in the direction inside/outside.

The maturational process, or rather the capacity to become what we are, is inborn and develops into the self, understood as a progressive organisation and realisation of the Ego, achieved through self-awareness. Therefore according to Winnicott, the self indicates the whole person and their self-representation. The self, its continuity and development give meaning to the individual's actions and life, which unfolds from an original dependence and immaturity through to independence and personal autonomy.

One of the functions of the self is mentally to work through sensory experiences to transform them into what will become the person's *psychic reality*. We achieve a sense of personal integrity in those moments when we perceive ourselves as whole beings and think: "I am". Self-awareness is what allows us to feel personal continuity, inasmuch as we are children, first, then adults and lastly old people, albeit still able to preserve a sense of cohesion. Everything changes, but the connecting thread remains the same.

Of course self-cohesion is the outcome of a process of integration, which occurs gradually, through back and forward movements. Moreover, we acquire our awareness of continuity and personal meaning in the context of a relationship, in other words, what is necessary is the presence of another, usually a good enough mother, able to understand the infant's needs. In the infant, in fact, self-cohesion is still labile. There can be times when infants struggle to recover their self-cohesion. At times it is not easy for them to recover their identities and re-enter their bodies, as, for instance, is the case upon waking from a deep sleep. Mothers, who know this intuitively, wake their children up gradually, before picking them up, so as to prevent them feeling panicky or anxious.

According to Winnicott, human beings experience primary anxieties such as a *threat of annihilation*, falling into pieces, falling forever, having no relation to one's body, being lost in space and having no means of communication whatsoever.

Moreover, the maturational process entails acceptance of the "not-me" and a capacity to relate to the external world. In this phase of self-development, the external world can appear as dangerous. Therefore, to be able to consolidate further, the self remains in a subjective space, based on illusion and omnipotence, both useful and necessary to achieve a sense of going on being. Infants know that external reality exists independently of them, yet they need to believe that the world belongs to them, or better still that they have created it. The baby's fantasy must meet external reality, represented by the mother's response.

Winnicott thinks that the experience of illusion is essential to the creation of the *potential space* of the self and so must not be destroyed by the mother's response. By supporting the baby's illusion, the mother allows it to experience objects in a paradoxical manner, both as subjectively created and objectively perceived, at the same time. This illusory dimension is clearly essential for the infant's perception of the continuity of its own being.

Winnicott turns Freud's theories upside down. Whilst Freud sees omnipotence as an illusory and narcissistic feature, Winnicott shows that an initial experience of boundless illusion is not only developmentally necessary, but also a foundation for our mental well-being.

To my mind, Winnicott's thought is of fundamental importance, when we try to understand the questions of subjective time and sense of future, but also to see the theme of separation anxiety and loss from a different angle.

Christopher Bollas (1989) gives an original reading of some of Winnicott's intuitions in relation to the issues of loss and subjective future. He thinks that, as people have an unconscious perception of the development of their own self, the inability to think about the future represents a particular type of loss. The most obvious instance of this is when a child loses a parent and thus loses the relationship with his/her own future. A parent's death implies not only the loss of a loved one, but also an impediment to "using" the parental object. In this case, damage occurs to the articulation of the self, which takes place through the object. Moreover all the *future options,* linked to the good objects and good relationships with them, are inevitably destroyed.

What is then the pain felt by the child or the adolescent who loses those future options? One could think about it as a loss of *potential self,* grief for what could have been, but will not be.

Understandably the anxiety and anger caused by this loss are enormous. There is rage for being struck by *fate*, rather then *destiny*.

Bollas understands *fate* as the feeling of not being free and authentic, but, rather, moved by the obscure and unknown forces of life. Conversely, *destiny* is the realisation of the subject's specific potential, which the author from the British psychoanalytic tradition defines as *idiom,* that is, an unconscious preconception inscribed in our psyche which spurs us to fulfil our creative talents. People who have an inner faith in their destiny develop an intuitive knowledge of the object relations necessary to the unfolding of their personal idiom.

Only by emotionally investing the future, can we fully make use of the determination and creative aggression necessary to create the most favourable conditions for our development.

I hope I have made it clear how Bollas, developing Winnicott's intuitions, puts forward a notion of mourning quite different from Freud's (1915 d) and Abraham's (1924). Whilst Freud and Abraham emphasise the pain and rage caused by the loss of the loved one, whose death frustrates the subject's omnipotent fantasy of eternal possession of the object, Bollas regards every loss as a painful limitation of the potential development of the self. To clarify further, the self can only develop within the context of object relations and therefore these object ties are necessary to the subject's psychic *osmosis*, inasmuch as they are a source of future options.

Bollas maintains that the mother's capacity to function as a support to her infant's omnipotent illusion of creativity combines with the destiny drive, thus founding and structuring the child's sense of self-development in time. This helps us imagine the meaning of the inner feeling of personal development in space and time.

People with an internal sense of their destiny drive will instinctively choose objects that will facilitate access to their future developmental potential. When they lose these objects, the consequence will be not only loss of the self, but also an obliteration of their potential self-development and future vision, in other words, Bollas' notion of destiny. Experiencing our life as meaningful is closely liked to this potential space, seen as developing in time, which allows us to be free of the temporal and spatial limits of life and to continuously invest our future projects, ambitions, aims and desires.

Should we possibly consider this space of illusion and unlimited potential in the same way as Freud's unconscious idea of immortality, of which he was so critical, being the realist scientist he was? The potential space, albeit merely an "illusion", is the transitional area necessary for our life projects and hopes.

According to Winnicott, psychosis is an illness caused by *environmental deficiencies*, first experienced by the subject when, as an immature infant in the phase of absolute dependence, s/he suffered the deprivation of vital and indispensable environmental provisions. Winnicott's hypothesis is that the fear of death and illness reactivates the primitive terror of the disintegration of the self amidst chaos and nothingness. The environmental provision of the potential space of illusion would thus represent the only means available to circumscribe, delimit and deny one's awareness of death.

There is no subjective self without the notion of development. The potentially infinite development, based upon the illusion of unlimited growth, is a constituent characteristic of the self. We can feel alive only if we can project ourselves into the future: this illusion is the background symphony that allows us to go on living.

What happens when we are faced with death, when the potential space is threatened with disintegration? The answer is that we should confront, at this point without illusion and defences, the experience of the end of our life. Death, in whatever way and at whatever age faces us, evokes in us terror similar to the anxieties of psychotic illness, comparable to psychic death. Even though we are aware of death, we still consider it an unthinkable occurrence. To make it thinkable, we would need to turn it into an object of our life enhancing curiosity, and essentially project it into a temporal and subjective dimension, which is necessary to enable us to have an experience and remember it.

An essential function of curiosity links it to memory, which employs it to explore both time past and time future. Conversely, death involves the loss of subjective time and memory function. Consequently, the loss of self, as an inseparable mind-body unity, can only feel like an irreparable absence.

Our religious imagery has the capacity to comfort us, as it is universally shared, but more importantly, it provides one of the possible solutions to the unthinkable. Stating that the individual's existence transcends the end of life, religion rescues the self, projecting it into a timeless future, where the potential space is preserved. Within this framework, there is only a temporary, rather than an absolute loss. (2)

NOTES

(1) According to Freud, the ego is primarily a body-ego (see *The Ego and the Id,* 1922).

(2) It would be interesting to study how religious systems deal with the problem of the loss of self which death brings about. That, however, is beyond the scope of this work. Christian religion guarantees the continuity and permanence of the individual self through the survival of the body and the soul. The doctrine of reincarnation contemplates also the rebirth of the bodily self, as it is a constituent part of the individual's identity. Conversely in Buddhism, after many rebirths, the self is at last obliterated and dissolved into nothingness, this being the ultimate solution to the anxiety of living and being reborn. In this case, the proposed solution "mortifies" the self in the literal sense of the term, to reconcile it with death, in a final and total acceptance of the disappearance of the self. It looks as if the two religions try to solve the immanent question of life and death, permanence and disappearance of the self, by erasing one of the two sides of the problem.

7

A HIGHER LEVEL OF CONSCIOUSNESS

Who would be so besotted as to die, without having made, at least, the round of this, his prison?
                       Marguerite Yourcenar, *The Abyss*

Ironically, the self is the last thing
to be understood by his possessor, even
after the possession of a theory of
consciousness.
                 Gerald M. Edelman, *Bright Air, Brilliant Fire:*
                             On the Matter of the Mind

Winnicott's intuition about the self, described in the previous chapter, helps us to understand why human beings cannot live without a sense of development of their existential personal space. Whenever this expectation of development and potential vitality is no longer available, we may still be alive, but our psychic life comes to an end or else an unspeakable pain clouds our mind. This is the same pain that depressed and some psychotic patients experience: the sense of potential self disappears and a painful feeling of not being alive takes its place.

Only a sense of self allows us to feel that we belong to the vital potential of the universe. This is the only way we can keep in contact with life and, secondarily, with death, too. To fully be a human being and to perceive oneself to be such, is predicated upon the notion of developmental time, which runs throughout life. This level of consciousness seems to be unavailable to other animals.

In this regard, Nietzsche writes in his work *On Use and Abuse of the History of Life* (1973):

> Observe the herd which is grazing besides you, it does not know what yesterday or tomorrow is. It springs around, eats, rests, digests, jumps up again, and so on from the morning to night and from day to day, with its likes and dislikes, closely tied to the peg of the moment and thus neither melancholy nor weary (...)
>
> One day a man demands of the beast: "Why do you not talk to me about your happiness, and only gaze at me?" The beast wants to answer, too and says: "That comes because I always immediately forget what I wanted to say". But by then the beast has already forgotten this reply and remains silent; so that the man wonders on once more, but he also wonders about himself, that he is not able to learn how to forget and that he always hangs on to past things. No matter how fast he runs, this chain runs with him".

In what way, then, are other animals different from human beings, who cannot forget and need to constantly bear in mind the passing of time? To try and answer this question, I will employ the neuroscientific framework put forward by Edelman (1993), who examines that mysterious human function we define as consciousness.

Edelman suggests that we should make a distinction between *primary consciousness* and *higher-level consciousness*. The former would indicate the awareness of worldly things: in this case, we have mental images of the present, but what is missing is the feeling of being a person with a past and a future.

On the other hand, a higher level of consciousness would involve a capacity to acknowledge one's actions and feelings; so it would include a sense of personal identity, with a present, a past and a future. Moreover, this more complex function would reveal our direct and self-reflective awareness of mental events, which take place outside the domain of our sensory organs or receptors. As human beings, we are aware of being aware.

Edelman proposes the concept of *qualia* to indicate the perceptions characteristic of the higher level of consciousness, only the individual experiencing subject can be aware of. As *qualia* cannot be fully shared with an observer, it is not possible to found a phenomenological psychology as an object of scientific communication like physics are. Not only can *qualia* not be communicated directly, but also, as it happens, any attempt to clarify them, inevitably alters them in unforeseeable ways.

Qualia are normally ignored in scientific procedures, because they could alter the objectivity of our observations; they cannot, however, be ignored in an inquiry into consciousness.

Edelman suggests that *the presence of qualia distinguishes a higher-level consciousness from primary consciousness*. It is only the former that endows the speaking person with a direct self-awareness and with a sense of subjective life, which can be relived and narrated. Conversely, primary consciousness, formed by phenomenal experiences and time-bound to the measurable present, lacks the concepts of past and future and is restricted to a brief memory span focused on a time interval, which Edelman defines as present. To be more precise, it is a *remembered present*. Lacking an explicit notion of a personal self, primary consciousness cannot shape the past and the future, as component parts of a temporal sequence.

An animal equipped with primary consciousness is able to see only the well-lit parts of a room; it can explicitly perceive and locate in the remembered present solely the objects emerging from the dark. This does not mean that the animal, merely endowed with primary consciousness, would not be capable of long-term memory and would not use it as a foundation for its actions. Clearly this is the case, but generally speaking, the animal is unaware of it and is unable to represent its own future life, making use of its memory to imagine itself in a time yet to come. To be able to do so, one needs access to language and the use of symbols, both being acquisitions pertaining to the higher level of consciousness.

According to Edelman, the subjective perception of emotions (*qualia*) belongs to the realm of consciousness of the self. (1) As a neuroscientist, he cannot describe, as a psychoanalyst would, the importance of the language of affect and the maternal responsiveness for the recognition and internalisation of emotions, as well as for the development of the sense of self. He goes as far as stating that a pattern of self-non self interaction may have preceded the acquisition of language proper.

Animals endowed with primary consciousness are unable to internalise the sense of time through affective knowledge; therefore their experience is purely linked to the concrete succession of events, which cannot be lived in an emotionally meaningful time.

The higher-level consciousness characteristic of human creatures (the psychoanalytic self) frees our thinking from its links with the immediate present and permits self-reflective awareness of our emotional life.

Edelman's inquiry allows us to understand why only human beings, equipped with a special vision of time and personal identity, have the capacity to represent death and in so doing, are exposed to anxieties unknown to other living species.

Only our awareness of time as emotionally significant, an exquisitely human prerogative, enables us to wonder about the temporal limits of our life. The representation of death as a possible occurrence in the future and not simply in the immediate present, is made possible by the complex experience of subjective time only human creatures have acquired. Even though we share with the rest of the animal kingdom the ability to be alerted by an external danger, we are unique in so far as we have acquired an inner sense of our finite nature. This drives us to ask questions and provide answers to the enigma of our personal destiny.

It is rather improbable that the experience of illness overburdens other animals with the psychic pain of anxiety, besides the physical suffering, as it is the humans' lot. Only the human subject asks: "What is happening to me, now? Could I be dying?" Also we are unique in wondering what our destiny will be after our death.

The remembered present, unlike the higher level consciousness, protects animals from the anxiety ensuing from our self-awareness; yet we cannot completely rule out the possibility that animals are capable of some form of awareness of their own death.

We inhabit the present, the past and the future whilst other living creatures live only in the present.

NOTE

(1) "With this view of higher level consciousness it is possible to see roughly what lies beneath the self that connects phonology to semantics in naming a sentence. Once a self is developed through social and linguistic interactions on a base of primary consciousness, a world is developed that requires naming and intending. This world reflects inner events that are perceptually experienced. Tragedy becomes possible-the loss of self by death or mental disorder, the remembrance of unassugeable pain".

8

IVÀN I'LÌC'S DEATH

> I know I will die, but I do not believe it.
> Jacques Madaule, *Considérations de la mort*

> There is little to be said. We are all fixed on a nice notion of ourselves, in good faith. However, Monsignor, while you keep still, clinging to your holy cassock with both hands, from your sleeve something slides away, slithering away like a snake, and you do not even notice it. It is life, Monsignor!
> Luigi Pirandello, *Henry IV*

The protagonist of Tolstoy's novel *The Death of Ivàn I'lìc* is a successful man. The second child of a modest family, he dies at the age of forty-five, having lived a "simple and ordinary" life. He is a witty and pleasant man.

During his childhood and adolescence, which go by and do not leave behind any significant marks, Ivàn gets accustomed to some of his own actions, originally he had felt ashamed and unhappy about, and concludes that they conform to the norm. In the course of his Law studies, he turns into an affable student, well able to perform his academic duties. He is not overtly servile, but is attracted to people of higher social status.

After his graduation, he leaves for the provincial town where he has a post as a governmental official. After some time, he accepts to move to another post he is promoted to and does not show any signs of regret or sorrow for the loss of the relationships he has made. He feels very much fulfilled by his position as an investigating magistrate; he is excited at the realisation that even the most important people are under his authority. After a couple of years, he meets an intelligent and brilliant young woman. When he understands she is in love with him, he tells himself: "Why should I not get married?"

With the birth of his first child, whom he duly looks after, the need to immerse himself in a world outside his family becomes ever more compelling. The more demanding his wife becomes, the more emotionally involved he gets in his work. Still, his wish to please his wife and meet her expectations lead him to apply for a reassignment and so he moves to a new town, on his own. In these circumstances Ivàn I'lìc, totally unprepared, meets his death, when he climbs on a ladder to check some curtains, falls down and hits his hip against a handle. He is not seriously injured but has a painful hip. The real illness manifests itself as a strange taste in the mouth and some abdominal trouble, located in the left side, the one affected by the trauma.

At this point, Ivàn goes from doctor to doctor, in a series of unsatisfactory encounters, because physicians examine and scrutinise him, tell and do not tell. His mood gets progressively worse; he comes to the conclusion that he is in serious trouble, whilst doctors and everyone else seem not to care. After yet another medical appointment, he returns home, where his wife's hurried and slightly bored insouciance leads him to trivialise and deny the seriousness of his condition. Thus, he concludes that perhaps he is suffering from just a minor ailment bound to disappear soon; yet his feeling that he is affected by something serious becomes more and more certain and oppressive.

> Ivàn I'lìc knew he was dying, and not only had he not become accustomed to that thought, but he simply could not understand it, as he could not comprehend that kind of thing.

He was unable to comprehend how death could happen to him, precisely himself, just when he was living a life of habits and pleasant memories. Not to anyone else, but to himself indeed.

> That example of syllogism he had studied in Kizevetter's logics: "Caius is a man, men are mortal, Caius is mortal", all throughout his life had seemed right but solely in relation to Caius, and completely meaningless as far as he was concerned. That was Caius, the man, man in general, and that sentence was absolutely right; but he was not Caius and was not man in general (. . .)

> It is death. Yes, it is death. And none of them know, or want to know, and have no compassion (. . .) To them it is a meaningless event, but they will die, too. They are stupid! I shall die first, but they will later: it will be the same for hem. And in the meantime, they enjoy themselves. Animals!

If, at this point, Ivàn I'lìc had been able to take into the grave with him the whole world, he did not want to leave behind, and all his relatives, who were detaching themselves from him, he would have been triumphant and satisfied. On the other hand, was his family not the mirror of his emotional indifference, emptiness and wish not to be disturbed by the pain of the world? The drama, which had been in store for a long time, explicitly unfolds only when Ivàn I'lìc, just a few hours before his death, as he mirrors himself in his family, discovers that his life was a failure, based, as it was, on falsification.

In his family he sees himself, all he had ever lived for, and understands that his life was an enormous (self) deception:

> If I were to die, knowing that I have wasted all that I had been given, if it were not possible to put it right, what would it then be like?

Ivàn I'lìc finally understands his drama only when he realises that he would have been helped if someone had expressed their love or noticed his dismay. Gerasim, his peasant servant was the only one to take care of him with humble solicitude, when asked.

It is too late when Ivàn I'lìc understands the value of human solidarity and also how much he has lost in life: there is no more time left to live, to repair and build a life on different values. Now, with this lacerating intuition, he is overwhelmed by inner chaos and despair. He lashes out his inhuman rage, screaming without pause, similarly to the desperate scream in Munch's painting, for three whole days, until everything quietens out in the silence of death.

It looks as though, before his illness, Ivàn never thought about the meaning of life: perhaps he imagined he would live a happy life with no time boundaries. We might wonder how he had come to the verge of an existential crisis, which, for him, at the age of forty-five, coincides with his own death. What did he think about it before? He seems to have located the thought of death outside his horizon and outside time. Yet he had already lost his parents and should have been somewhat worried, regarding that event as the beginning of the descending course of his own life.

Ivàn I'lìc, an efficient judge, able to find balanced and brilliant solutions, had had but a limited ability to think and certainly he had shown little awareness of his feelings. He had never fallen in love, or had shown passionate feelings to anyone. He had performed well and dutifully in his work, without any emotional upset.

We could say that his life had been well functioning, but this is precisely the problem he had been unaware of. Everything seemed to have happened naturally, with no bad faith or deceit on his part. However, even without the stressful irruption of his illness, sooner or later Ivàn I'lìc's life would have been perturbed by the thought of old age and death.

What memories, what relationships or experiences could he evoke, to feel comforted and give meaning to his life? A life lived by his egocentric greed could only be felt as empty and meaningless.

> I shall be no more, but what will there be then? There will be nothing. And where shall I be, when I am no more? Could I be dying? No, I do not want to.

Tolstoy's short novel may be seen as a lucid metaphor for the anxiety of the mid-life crisis. In this circumstance, people may become aware that the best part of their life has irreparably gone and they may realise they have wasted it and they have no more time to remedy and save things. This is why some people, who have led "normal", successful and even happy lives, enter their mid-life, experiencing an inexplicable existential malaise. Clearly, they are anguished because they are ill equipped to face the second half of their lives.

9

THE MID-LIFE CRISIS

The terror of death is the most telling sign
of a false, that is bad, life.
                       Ludwig Wittgenstein, *Notebooks 1914-16*

I know pretty well, said Elias, that I have reached
the end of my life, but I am convinced that I am just
beginning my work. Death is not frightening for those
who can see a meaning in their life and nothing is more
meaningful than an incomplete piece of work.
           F. Cavalli, preface to *The Loneliness of the Dying*
                                        by Norbert Elias

The psychoanalyst Elliott Jacques, in an important paper entitled "Death and middle-life crisis" (1965), attempts to explain why people find it difficult to face the thought of their own death. His theoretical contribution is inspired by Melanie Klein, who thinks that the subjective experience of death is linked to the primitive anxieties characteristic of our individual relational patterns with the internal and external world.

  Jacques' definition of mid-life crisis applies to that particular age, between thirty and forty, that leads to a process of psychological transformation, variable from person to person and whose duration is undefined. This is a critical phase in everyone's life cycle. With some artists, this crisis can result in profound changes in creative work.

Jacques maintains that, in the course of the middle-life crisis, people move away from their initial idealism and come to a more realistic, intimate and thoughtful world view. Moreover, he regards the idealism characteristic of the first half of life as founded on the denial of two essential aspects of our existence: the inevitability of our death and the awareness of our destructive drives. An explicit acceptance of these two features of our inner world would be the indispensable premise to enable us to overcome our mid-life crisis and move on to the age of maturity.

When people can face their inborn destructiveness as well as the prospect of their own death, the quality and contents of their creative output can change.

Jacques observes that, when we come to "the middle of the journey of our life", what might seem simple from a chronological point of view, reveals itself to be complex as far as one's emotions are concerned.

This is the time when people stop growing and start aging. They have already lived the first phase of their life; often they have a family, work and elderly parents. The essential task of this age seems to be the achievement of full adulthood. This is clearly a paradoxical existential experience, in that we enter the fullness of life, whilst, at the same time, we become more and more aware of its finiteness. Consequently death no longer appears to be just a generic concept or somebody else's experience, rather it concerns us personally, as we come to think of our own, all too real mortality.

Until this point, we might have seen life as an endless upward movement, towards a far-reaching horizon. On the contrary, now we feel we have reached the top of a hill, from which we commence our descent towards the end, which is still far away, nevertheless inevitable.

Awareness of our mortality triggers depressive feelings and infantile anxieties re-emerge. The thought of a life leading towards death is akin to an intense, unconscious psychic disturbance, similar to a depressive breakdown. One's own death is felt to be like chaos, confusion and persecution. To be able to establish fulfilling relationships, both in the internal and external world is closely linked to the capacity to struggle with the inner chaos successfully and to maintain a rapport with the good objects.

If the balance between love and hate leans towards the latter, destructiveness manifests itself fully as self-destructiveness, envy, grandiose omnipotence, cruelty, narcissism and greed. The breakdown threatening middle age can temporarily be avoided strengthening the defences that keep depression at bay. These defences may include one's deliberate efforts to look younger, relying, for instance, on sexual fantasies that compensate for the underlying sense of loss of vitality.

These are just vain attempts to defy the passage of time and they may lead to an emotional impoverishment or to character deterioration.

People can overcome their mid-life crisis only if they succeed in facing constructively the notion of the limits of life and the traumatic impact of the thought of death. When this experience evolves in a positive way, the second half of life can be lived usefully and productively. We know that working through the pain caused by our finite human nature is not accomplished once for all, rather it is an ongoing process. After a certain age, the work of mourning is a constant feature of our psychic life.

After the age of fifty or sixty, we understand ever more clearly that we cannot expect dramatic changes and that we need to complete what we have begun. Indeed, it is not easy, at this age, to open up to new perspectives and ambitions. The feeling that our horizon becomes ever more limited can be ameliorated if we are able to reflect on how much we can still create and transmit to those who will come after us.

At this point I will describe my psychoanalytic work with a patient and try to show the anxieties of a mature person grappling with her "mid-life crisis". With this clinical material I would like to demonstrate how psychoanalytic working through could help a person acquire the inner resources to deal adequately with the aging process. In the absence of these inner resources, death can only be seen as utter loss, bleak loneliness and a perturbing manifestation of the unknown.

The patient in question is forty-nine. She has had a few hospital admissions for her depressive illness and, during one of these admissions; Electric Shock Treatment was performed on her. She is married and has a son. She lives with her husband, with whom she has had no significant emotional relationship for a long time. On his instigation, their sexual relationship has come to an end.

The patient comes from a more modest social class than her husband's and seems to have chosen a socially convenient marriage.

She comes into analysis, as she will acknowledge some time later, because she is concerned about the possible ending of an extramarital relationship, as indeed will happen during treatment.

The patient is grappling with her awareness that she has to face the second half of her life, accompanied by a profound sense of her destructiveness and consequent guilt.

She is approaching her 50s: her son, the object of her devotion and great idealisation, has recently decided to leave home.

Her anxiety is very well expressed through the first dream of her analysis:

> I am in a Mediterranean town; I am arrested and accused of being too elegant; I am on a road that goes who knows where (. . .) there is one more building and a church, but in reality there is just the front of the church, like in a theatre scenario.

She associates the church with the one where she got married; the town is where she went on her honeymoon.

A few months into the analysis, having discovered that her husband has an affair, the patient, very reluctantly, forces herself to separate from him, when she realises that he does not intend to stop the relationship with his lover. At this time violent feelings of jealousy and resentment emerge with such intensity as to result in a suicide attempt.

Throughout these experiences, the patient sees herself as the "victim of her husband", and is totally unable to acknowledge her own contribution to, and responsibility for, the failure of her marriage. She completely denies her own unfaithfulness to her husband, since the early days of the marriage.

In the transference, a sado-masochistic relationship becomes apparent very quickly. The patient accuses me of innumerable faults, cruelties or omissions and often she launches violent tirades against me. She endlessly challenges the analytic boundaries, raising objections against session times, holidays or my fees. She experiences my analytic attitude as a repeated practice of cruelty: if I do not make interpretations, she thinks it is because I wish to humiliate her, if I do give them, it is only to make her feel horrible. She sees me as the analyst who wants to deprive her of her pleasures, of her relationship with her partner or with other men, with whom she has occasional encounters and will ultimately change her into a nun.

Clearly the patient has an extremely cruel relationship with her object, whilst, at the same time, she attributes to it her guilt for her own sadism. Externalisations of this sado-masochistic object relation occur with me in the analysis and with her family in her external life. In this phase, she needs to use the analysis to meet her need to have someone who can tolerate the projection of her responsibility and guilt.

In the countertransference, I find it unusually difficult to feel any sympathy or warmth for her. The patient and myself seem to be stuck in a quarrelsome relationship, in danger of repeating, in the transference, the "pattern" of her early interactions with her parents, repeated later on with her husband.

Internally, however, she is the one who feels blamed by a parent who reproaches her for her inability to love and make reparation. This internal state is linked to her infantile experience with her father, whom she regarded as the only parent she could respect. He was the only one who looked after the family and, at the same time, encouraged her to do well in her academic studies, first, and in her work, later. Her mother, an affectionate, but insensitive woman, was prone to sudden, angry outbursts, often hysterically depressed and completely dependent on her husband. From the patient's childhood memories, it appears that her father was a very strict person. Her 'internal father' accuses her of being incompetent and worthless. However this internal father, the patient states, has an Achilles' heal, in that he is sexually interested in her. (1)

The super-ego introject is contradictory and confusing, inasmuch as it exalts and excites her, making her feel special, only to attack and denigrate her, thus eliciting uncertainty and confusion in her. For example, during the separation from her husband, her mind oscillates between images of herself as a wife brutally humiliated by her husband and its opposite, a selfish woman, who has abandoned and sacrificed her son and her spouse. (2) This super-ego structure imposes extreme oscillations, thus causing disequilibrium in the patient's psychic life. Slowly, though, in the analysis, the atmosphere charged with excitement, persecution and projection of her guilty feelings, relaxes.

At the same time as she experiences a renewed good relationship with the world, feeling no longer full of envy and destructive wishes, she has a dream where

> I look at my hands and realise that my ring finger, which had broken, was repaired and healed.

The patient's brother appears in her associations. He had a finger amputated when a bomb, found in the back garden, exploded, at the end of the Second World War. Identified with her brother, she tells herself, in the dream, that there is something left and she can still use her remaining fingers. Also she has associations to her marriage, allowing more friendly feelings towards her husband to emerge. Moreover she can feel remorse for what she has lost in her life so far, because of the domination of a 'capricious and false' part of her. This makes it possible for her to take stock of her life in a more balanced and realistic way, valuing more what she does have. After five years' analysis this new more harmonious mode of relating consolidates, both in her external world and in her communication with me.

Going back to the reasons contributing to the patient's decision to seek analytic help, I intend to explore in detail the anxieties, fears and wishes, somewhat typical in people who come to analysis at a later age.

When she first contacted me on the telephone, with a view to start an analytic treatment, she soon posed the question of her age and asked: "Is it possible to have an analysis at my age?"

As I will clarify later, the question of age in analysis has not only practical, but also complex theoretical implications. Is it possible to hope for changes of the personality structure at a certain age, or should we think, as Freud did, that inertia characterises the mental functioning of people nearing old age?

If we listen carefully to the patient just described, this question acquires a more specific meaning, in that, in reality, she is asking whether she has enough time to re-build a more authentic identity, which could help her to face the last part of her life, or whether she should regard her life as stuck in the past and failed.

Her first dream contains an account of the factors underlying her breakdown, as well as the reasons why she seems unable to see a possible re-construction. In this dream, in fact, the patient is accused of having been too elegant, in other words, of having sacrificed the true values of life to her vanity. She is an attractive, lively and intelligent woman, whose life has been successful. She married a wealthy and well-to-do man and was possibly driven into the marriage by the influence of her family environment. Therefore she accepted to marry a man she did not love and started to feel estranged from, soon after the wedding.

For a long time, she thought she could go on as she was. Although she suffered periodic bouts of depression, she did not link them to her life choices and she was completely unaware of her malaise, which therefore remained unconscious. Thinking of herself as an attractive, intelligent and lively woman, the mother of a son she could love and admire and who could make her feel young and alive all the time, had offered her some compensation for her sense of existential futility.

Her crisis becomes apparent at the time when the patient begins to understand that she can no longer regard herself as attractive because of her advancing age, just when her son is about to leave home and her lover is losing interest in her. What inner resources can she find within herself and rely on, at this point, to face the rest of her life? In the dream, the vision of her superficial and false life choices, especially her marriage, which is just a facade, turns into an irreversible and hopeless condemnation.

We know from her history that her relationship with her mother had not been satisfactory. The mother herself had been incapable of facing life and valuing it. Her father had provided a better role model and had shown her a possible avenue of development, encouraging her to succeed in her studies. At the same time, though, he had idealised her to the point of making her excessively dependent on her physical beauty. Her father's attitude must have somewhat contributed to the patient's feeling of being special and being able to live above everyone else, unperturbed by the usual difficulties of living. This illusion of superiority suddenly crashed in the course of her mid-life crisis.

We could ask ourselves: if the patient has grown up with the notion that she was accepted and desired solely for her physical attractiveness, how can she hope to be loved and understood when she loses it? What future is there for her?

The patient is married to a man who chose her when she was very young and she has continued to believe that her husband would always desire her. On the contrary, during her analysis, she has discovered that this was not the case, that he also had a lover and was interested in other women. This discovery was intolerable for her. In the dream the patient talks about her life as a kind of faked scenario. Being fake permeates many aspects of her life and this is yet another reason why she is not at all convinced that she might be able to lead a more authentic life.

In this case the mid-life crisis destroys old equilibriums and defences; the patient is compelled to begin treatment precisely because she has no prospect to build something which might sustain her in the second half of her life. Coming for analysis opens up for her the possibility of creating a new structure. With hindsight, we can see how the analytic experience has allowed her to move forward in this direction.

The advent of the "mid-life crisis" does not always present as a breakdown of "successful" defences of fraudulence. For some people the request for psychoanalytic help in their mature age implies a wish to acquire finally an equilibrium not only suitable to work through this stage of their life, but also to achieve real aliveness. These are cases of people who have been deprived of the favourable conditions for psychological growth and so they realise they are aging even before they have had the opportunity to develop their life.

A forty-six year old male patient comes for treatment with this presentation. He suffers from panic crises, thinking of death, too. He remembers that even as a child he was tormented by this problem, to the point of being unable to sleep on his own. At present his anxiety states occur upon waking up. He is seized by the sudden fear that he has no more time left and that his life is over, before he has a chance to live it fully. It is as if he could not think realistically about his life span, seeing himself, actually, beyond any time boundaries or constraints. Then, suddenly, his defensive denial decreases, giving way to the thought of his impending death and he is overwhelmed by a panic state.

He has begun with me his second analysis. He was married, is now separated and childless. His previous relationships have been disappointing. He had chosen older partners, who ended up devaluing him, regarding him as inadequate and finally leaving him. He is not, however, a cold person or someone without merit; quite the opposite, he has an emotional and ideal world he seems unable to value.

So far he has chosen female partners more mature and self-assured than himself, to whom he has never really been emotionally or sexually attracted, hampered by his intrinsic insecurity. In reality, his need to be stimulated or even guided by other people seems to have been the predominant feature of these relationships.

In one of the early sessions of his analysis, he reports a dream where

> he is on a train, stationery on a dead-end track, then someone drives a lorry and he is beside the driver; finally he is in a car where he is in the driver's seat.

Associating to the dream, he states that one of the aims of this new psychoanalytic adventure is the project of being in the driver's seat of his own life.

In the course of his analysis, he appears more and more concerned that he might not be able to establish a successful meaningful relationship, which would protect him from the inexorable perspective of a lonely old age.

He thinks he got everything wrong in his life, even the choice of his profession, which, on the other hand, he performs successfully and competently. Yet he thinks he will carry on with his profession, out of necessity, rather than out of interest.

A profound anxiety that he will be stuck in this state, grow old and die, without achieving vitality or fulfilment torments him, keeps him awake at night and soon becomes the leitmotiv of the analysis.

The patient believes that a sudden enlightenment should transform his life and this is what he would like from the analysis; because of this firmly held conviction, he denies the significance of our relationship and analytic work. He realises that, as a consequence of his devaluation of our analytic work, he forgets and loses his thoughts from one session to another. The significant material emerging from the sessions, even though at the time it touches him, does not stay with him and does not provide a stimulus for his own personal elaboration and integration.

He begins one of his sessions stating that he had been thinking again about something I had said regarding our joint analytic work, which could take the place of his expectation of a transforming enlightenment. In reality I had told him that he seemed to perceive me as an "absent" father who did not actually look after him or share his experiences. He then acknowledged having no sense of a paternal presence, inside. He had a non-existent relationship with his father, who died when the patient was still quite young. His father would come back home after his long business trips, immerse himself in his hobbies and have no intimate relationship with him.

Faced with the difficulties of his relationship with his mother, basically depressed and childishly dependent on her husband, he elected to look for guidance outside his family and began to have erotic relationships with more mature women. How could he have internalised a paternal ideal, grown up and taken care of his own loved ones, in turn?

Reflecting on his work, he realises that he prefers consultancy, rather than senior executive positions, which would force him to assume larger responsibilities.

He becomes aware that the absence of a healthy dependent relationship with his father, in childhood, has prevented him from growing up with an understanding of the meaning of life. Perceiving his life as a failed opportunity is now a source of great anxiety and, consequently, any awareness of his finite human nature feels like an agonising claustrophobic enclosure.

Through the psychoanalytic encounter, this patient experiences a new mode of relating, which helps him to develop a sense of his own identity; but this acquisition is predicated upon his capacity to shed the narrow-mindedness and unconscious prejudice he has grown accustomed to. He is in pain, because some vital parts of him have been unacknowledged and constrained for too long, and now he needs to get in touch with them, if he wishes to develop new intuitive abilities, to make fully use of his personal talents and thus give meaning to his life.

NOTES

(1) On this basis, the patient employs her seductiveness to defend herself from the cruelty of her super-ego, but this strategy is, nonetheless, inadequate to change the quality of her internal object relation. Once the seduction has taken place, there is a consequent exacerbation of the super-ego's accusations, which are reiterated over and over again ("the patient is a whore . . .")

(2) The patient oscillates all the time between an ascetic-spiritual ideal (in the transference, the analyst preaches moral austerity) and an instinctual ideal (in a dream there is "the analyst with a bohemian hat" that colludes with her erotising fantasies; there is also an unmarried uncle who, in her childhood, made her feel like "his girl-friend").

10

PSYCHOANALYSIS IN OLD AGE

Death is inside us. It advances progressively.
Little by little things begin to look confused and
alike. Son, after a certain age, everything
feels the same and rather pointless.
                                Yasmina Reza, *Despair*

Let us endeavour so as to live that when we come to die
even the undertaker will be sorry.
       Mark Twain, *The Tragedy of Pudd'nhead Wilson
             and the Comedy of the Extraordinary Twins*

Freud was nearly fifty when he declared himself to be rather sceptical about psychoanalysis as a beneficial treatment for older people. He actually considered age a very important factor in assessing whether psychoanalytic treatment would be suitable and thought that there were at least two good reasons not to recommend it to people well on in their years. The first reason was that, around the age of fifty, the elasticity of mental processes decreases and so does the capacity to adapt to new situations. Consequently analysis cannot yield significant transformations. The second reason was that the older person had accumulated such a variety of memories and experiences that it would only be possible to work through them over a very long period of time. (1) Essentially Freud's views remained unchanged, and even later, in 1931; he reiterated that old age was a contraindication to analysis. The difficulty would be even greater for women, who, with age, become more rigid than men. Freud finally mentioned the question of older people's analysability in *Analysis Terminable and Interminable* (1937):

> In another group of cases we are surprised by an attitude in our patients, which can only be put down to a depletion of the plasticity, the capacity for change and further development, which we should ordinarily expect. (. . .) One finds the same thing in very old people, in which case it is explained as being due to what is described as a force of habit or an exhaustion of receptivity – a kind of psychical entropy.

As has been noticed, Freud's judgement appears rather ungenerous, and is also contradicted by his own life. Indeed his creativity manifested itself fully in his fifties and progressed, undiminished, well into his old age. Besides, there are passages of his writings, where he seemingly contradicts his own views about the rigidity of psychic development in old age. In *Beyond the Pleasure Principle,* (1920), in fact, he writes:

> We have learnt that unconscious mental processes are in themselves timeless. This means (. . .) that time does not change them in any way and that the idea of time cannot be applied to them.

Two American psychoanalysts, Harold and Mavis Wilie (1989), rightly observe that if we apply Freud's theory to analysts themselves, rather than just to their patients, we would be in a paradoxical situation. Seemingly we complete our lengthy and complex psychoanalytic training rather late, precisely at the age that Freud considered of little flexibility. Moreover, there are other factors, which need to be borne in mind. For instance, Nina Coltart, in her paper on the analytic psychotherapy of an older patient (1991), reported how she became interested in elderly people's problems, when she got older. (2) Furthermore, she makes the important observation that there is a noticeable difference for the analyst, when he or she analyses a person of the same age or younger, rather than someone older, who is going through complex experiences still unknown to the analyst. Therefore the older patient's treatment demands of the analyst a greater capacity for identification and empathy.

In retrospect, we could think that Freud's judgement was somewhat superficial and hasty, perhaps influenced by the common place, according to which old age exacerbates some character traits, like a caricature. Furthermore, I believe that Freud's conclusion was closely linked to his theory, which located the effectiveness of therapy in its capacity to help patients to re-live their early childhood complexes. Though this experience, a new self-awareness would emerge, enabling the patient to develop into adulthood. Yet, if childhood memories were so far away or if the quantity of later experiences was so great, how could the analytic process make headway? If the question was thus formulated, doubtfulness was the inevitable outcome.

Today, our conceptualisations of psychoanalytic therapy and technique are very different from the widely held views in Freud's times. Likewise, the current theories about our mental life have changed, but, above all, psychoanalytical theoretical models have changed. It was coherent with Freud's drive theory to think that instinctual energy was more alive and malleable in the early phases of life and less in later ones. If psychic maturation revolved around the Oedipus complex, how could the psychoanalyst think that a relatively older person could still address those long past emotional vicissitudes?

Freud's view of older people as unsuitable for psychoanalysis prevailed for a long time amongst the majority of psychoanalysts. Only occasionally have there been a few voices of disagreement, amongst them Karl Abraham's. In a paper written in 1919, "The Applicability of Psycho-Analytic Treatments to Patients at an Advanced Age", he expressed ideas that diverged from those prevailing at that time. In essence, Abraham reportes that amongst the psychoanalysts there was a widely held opinion that the outcome of analytic treatment of patients between thirty and forty was rather uncertain. Furthermore, the age between forty and fifty was a positive contraindication.

When Abraham first began his clinical practice, he also thought that analysis was not advisable later on in life. Only after long hesitations, did he accept to take into treatment relatively older patients, who explicitly requested it. He told himself that even though he might not be able to obtain successful therapeutic results with these patients, he would, at least, offer them his understanding and attention. On the basis of his own experience, Abraham maintains that not only can the analyses of elderly patients obtain good therapeutic results, but also some of them are amongst the most successful. Abraham states that the most favourable cases are those where the onset of symptoms occurred in middle age. Conversely, the worst outcome is observable in the analysis of those patients whose neurosis first manifested itself in youth or, sometime, even in childhood.

Therefore, the age of the neurosis is more important than the neurotic patient's age.

Naturally the analyst treats more easily the relatively recent psychopathological symptoms than the long-standing ones. Older persons, precisely because of their capacity for emotional resonance, in analysis can re-live their childhood and their past and can thus recover lost aspects of their emotional life. Clearly Abraham suggests that analysis can be useful in helping the person face the anxiety of old age.

If, indeed, we think about the existential crises that characterise the life cycle, and specifically old age, we can conceptualise them differently from Freud, with his drive theory. For instance, the theoretical model later developed by Melanie Klein, with its emphasis on the important role that unconscious phantasies play in causing anxiety, is more suitable to the analytic treatment of older patients. (3) Approaching old age and the prospect of facing one's own death can be particularly upsetting for some people, to the extent that they can shake defences, which until then have guaranteed a certain psychic equilibrium.

Only in the last few decades have psychoanalysts been interested in elderly people's life problems and in the possibility of taking them into analysis. Pearl King (1980) explores the reasons why a person might want to enter analysis in old age. Amongst the various reasons, there might be the fear of loss of sexual potency, the approaching retirement or the children's leaving home. People are very aware of the limits of their own life and with this knowledge comes the certainty that the desired aims, having been postponed, can no longer be achieved.

Also in favour of older people's analysability are Harold and Mavis Wilie (1987) who remind us that Freud's recommendation that psychoanalysts should continue their self-analysis indicates that there is no such a time limit to the process of growth and psychological development. Working through psychic conflicts is a life-long task; and the essential emotional issues regarding the Oedipus conflict, such as separation and mourning, re-emerge in every phase of the life cycle (marriage, childbirth, illness, retirement, old age or death).

Pollock (1982) considers psychoanalysis as a humanising force, enabling people to make contact with those neglected or split off parts of themselves, which continue to exert a powerful influence on their life and cause suffering. The analytic process revives these parts; affect-laden memories re-emerge and new modes of intimacy become available, regardless of the age of the patient. Many authors have described the vicissitudes of older patients' psychoanalytic therapies: Cohen, 1982; Coltart, 1991; Hinze, 1987; King, 1980; Pollock, 1982; Segal, 1958, to mention just a few.

Now I would like to refer to Hanna Segal's paper entitled "Fear of Death: Notes on the Analysis of an Old Man", as it demonstrates clearly how the constellation of defences put under strain and the feelings not worked through in the course of a person's life can cause a breakdown in the imminence of death.

Hanna Segal suggests that in many elderly patients an unconscious fear of death causes a psychotic breakdown. The patient she describes commences psychoanalytic treatment at the age of seventy-three and a half and terminates just before his seventy-fifth birthday. After a psychotic breakdown, his symptoms, in spite of intensive psychiatric care, had stabilised as hypochondria, depression and paranoid delusions. He lived abroad for a long time, and the precipitating factor in his breakdown was learning about the tragic death, that occurred in an extermination camp, of his family, from whom he had moved away in his youth. At the same time he learnt of the arrest of an agent whom he used to pay illegally to obtain some job orders. Even though the agent's arrest was unrelated to his transactions with him, the patient started to feel persecuted by the police, to see his name printed in the newspapers and to hear his case talked about on the radio.

The patient had memories of his mother as cold and rejecting, whilst he preserved an idealised picture of his father. After his father's death, the patient, who was then seventeen, fled Ukraine to settle down in Rhodesia, where he did rather well. All throughout those years, he held on to his resentment towards his mother, who, apparently, favoured his siblings. Repeating the idealised relationship with his father, he developed a strongly idealised bond with his own son. His son's wish for emancipation put strain on the relationship and precipitated the patient into psychosis.

Hanna Segal states that a large part of the analysis aimed at helping the patient to develop an awareness and acceptance of old age and death. As the patient went into analysis with the unconscious expectation that the treatment would give him back his lost youth, the work explored above all his relationship with his son, the supposedly ideal object who allowed him to see himself as ageless. Gradually, the patient came to realise that his son, however close to him he might have been, could not be a mirroring object. As an autonomous individual, he had his own life and future to look forward to. Reflecting back on his past, began to emerge feelings of guilt towards his family, he thought he had abandoned to themselves. Working through his feelings towards his mother, he realised how hard she must have worked to support the whole family when they were growing up. The pain for the approaching end of his life and for the analysis nearing termination accompanied his desire to return to Rhodesia to meet up with his old friends and re-join his family. Even though death was becoming nearer and nearer, he was still able to take pleasure in what was left of his life. He was then able to think about his children and grandchildren not as projections of parts of himself, but as separate people who would grow and go on living after his death. He returned to work and was able to look after his family and his wife when she became ill. The patient lived ten more years, after the ending of his analysis. Hanna Segal concludes her paper stating that the analytic work with this particular patient helped her modify some of her ideas about the prognosis of analysis in old age.

As we can see from the above-mentioned literature, psychoanalytic interest for the problems of middle and old age is far from negligible. The question of our transience, the necessity to give meaning to our life and understand what has not been possible to comprehend and integrate before, which I regard as the central issue of every analysis, comes up again in old age and with greater urgency, as we get nearer to the end of our days.

11

DEATH AND PSYCHOSIS

> In the presence of death, we all live in a city without walls.
>
> Epicurus, *Letters*

> Tragedy becomes possible: the loss of self by death or mental disorder.
>
> Gerald M. Edelman, *Bright Air, Brilliant Fire: On the Matter of the mind*

It is a widespread opinion that amongst the many forms of denial of reality to which psychotic patients resort, the disavowal of death is the most common. Patients deny not only their own death, but also the death of their family members. It is possible, however, to observe how, as they free themselves from their psychotic imprisonment, they come to accept the inevitability of their own death, which was an unthinkable and strenuously denied occurrence while they were ill.

Harold Searles (1961) is amongst the psychoanalysts who have explored the relationship between psychosis and death anxiety. He maintains that the terror associated with the perception of death is one of the main sources of anxiety against which psychosis provides a defence. The North American author thinks that

DEATH AND PSYCHOSIS

becoming psychotic is a compulsory choice in order *not to have to face* the fact of life of our finite nature, which is one of the many aspects of our internal and external reality. He describes a few clinical cases, which he regards as an appropriate illustration of his theory, whereas I would interpret them in a somewhat different way. Amongst the various cases of patients suffering from chronic psychosis, Searles describes in some detail a woman who successfully developed a realistic representation of herself and the world, after three and a half years of psychotherapy. The patient spent most of her time in the gardens of the hospital where she had been admitted, picking up fallen leaves, small birds and other little dead animals, which she tried to bring back to life by means of strange, magic alchemy practices. One could clearly understand that she thought of herself as God, intent on restoring life to dead things.

On an autumn day, the patient communicated without words her wistful, painful state of mind to her therapist, who was sitting next to her. Then, looking at the leaves, which she had picked up, with tears in her eyes, she said: "I cannot transform these leaves into something else, for example sheep". To this Searles replied: "Perhaps you are beginning to understand that human life is the same; life ends in death, just like these leaves". "Yes" acknowledged the patient. The patient's reply came across as an acceptance of some very important aspects of reality, which involved relinquishing the fantasy of being like God and acknowledging human beings' mortality. Searles adds that the patient was convinced that her parents were still alive, in spite of her knowledge of their death.

This very touching account leads us to think that the sense of omnipotence, in this case developed into a full blown delusion, could represent a defence against a painful awareness of death and emotional reality, but does not demonstrate, however, how the fear of death triggers psychotic symptoms. I wish to emphasise this last point because, even though this terror could be an important factor in the onset of the illness, it is nonetheless necessary, in every case, to investigate what the meaning of death might be in the psychotic experience of each patient.

A young analytic patient of mine seemed to have fallen ill precisely as a reaction to his fear of death. Soon after his graduation, he perceived with unbearable anxiety that he could die, without leaving any mark or memories of himself to others: he feared that if he were to die, there would be no one at his funeral. His psychotic episode occurred as a reaction to this dread. The patient began to develop a grandiose fantasy, and was convinced that he was destined for a brilliant career within the multinational company where he had just started work. He was certain that within a short time he would get to the world top management, and so everyone would revere him in that position.

This is also a case where the sense of omnipotence is deployed in the service of denial of the reality of death. But what do we mean by death, in this case? Working with this patient, it becomes clear that the deadly feeling relates to his psychic self, to the characteristic underlying insubstantiality and meaninglessness at the core of his being. In fact he was afraid that nobody would remember him. The creation of a mental state of omnipotence, immortality and megalomania, and the certainty of being God-like is precisely an attempt to fight off the terror of a psychic lack of being. (1)

Going back to Searles' patient, it does not appear to be so clear and unequivocal that her intention to restore life to dead objects, in her God-like state, was just an attempt to counteract her anguish about the prospect of her biological death. On the contrary, I think that the patient was omnipotently trying to re-create the lively parts of herself, to rescue them from the *psychic death* of psychosis. Whilst according to Searles the fear of death could trigger a psychotic state, I think, on the contrary, that *psychosis is death*. (2)

We can certainly assume that the fear of death is, in any case, especially disturbing for those patients who perceive in themselves, more acutely than others, a lack of vitality and hope in their psychic development, even before the onset of their illness. My hypothesis is that the psychotic, far from denying his or her death, is, on same level, very aware of it. Psychotic patients, in fact, seem to disprove what Freud stated so insistently, that death does not feature in dreams because its finite temporality cannot find a suitable representation in the timeless unconscious. In my experience, there are some dreams of psychotic patients, which contain the theme of death and through them they express their awareness that psychosis is death.

> The view was enchanting, but I looked down at the people working and the boats moving in the valley, with feelings that were dead to me, and I dead to them, and yet with that painful apprehension of a dream, that I was cut off from them by a charm, by a riddle I was every minute on the point of guessing.

Thus writes Perceval, a psychotic patient who successfully completed his journey back from madness and whose diary Gregory Bateson (1961) published.

Death appears very frequently in the dreams of psychotic patients (De Masi, 2001) and also it is often idealised. The idealisation of death helps to understand the confusion between what is alive and what is deadly, between fear of and fascination with psychic death, which is one of the fundamental problems of psychosis. For these reasons the terror of finally disappearing coincides with the psychotic's real anxiety. This anxiety refers to the destruction of the self and the loss of the symbolic universe, both of which are essential features of psychosis. Real death, perceived in moments when the patients' omnipotence collapses, becomes a source of persecution, because, at such times, their awareness of their psychic destruction and their incapacity to make reparation emerge. According to Melanie Klein (1963),

> The schizophrenic feels that he is hopelessly in bits and that he will never be in possession of his self. The sense of being surrounded by a hostile world, which is characteristic of the paranoid aspect of the schizophrenic illness, not only increases all his anxieties, but vitally influences his feeling of loneliness.

She reiterates in 1955:

> The schizophrenic feels that he is hopelessly in bits and that he will never be in possession of his self.

There is a link between the question of personal integrity and the capacity to face death: when integrity is lacking, anxieties increase.

In his work on schizophrenia and the inevitability of death, Searles (1961) comes to the same conclusions as Klein. He emphasises that every human being faces a dilemma: s/he cannot look death in the face if not a whole person, yet can become a whole person only when capable of looking death in the face. Schizophrenics encounter additional difficulties in attempting to resolve this dilemma: as long as s/he remains a schizophrenic, s/he lacks the necessary integrity to master this predicament. Only a relatively whole person can feel part of the integrity of humankind:

> In so far as an individual is a whole person intrapsychically, and able to participate wholly in his related-ness with other persons as well as with his non-human environment, he does not react to this subject of life's finitude as a separate nucleus of feelings in itself. It constitutes, rather, an ingredient of, or background for all his life-experiences. In so far as we can dare to keep ourselves open to the recognition of the finitude of our lives, this recognition can make our pleasurable experiences more precious, our despair more supportable, our work matter not of resented drudgery, but of wholehearted dedication, and so on. Just as one can be a truly whole person only through facing this harshest aspect of reality, the inevitability of death, so, too, can one become able to live fully, only if one lives in the light of this recognition.

Searles emphasises how important it is for psychoanalysts and psychotherapists to have a profound belief that life is meaningful and worth living, even though, sometimes, it can feel empty, futile and frightening at the prospect of death. In the face of the challenge and the pain of living, the achievement of the sense of personal integrity is one of the most complex aspects of human experience.

Landsberg (1936) reminds us that human uncertainty before death is due not only to a blank in biological sciences, but also to our inability to know our own destiny, and in this "ignorance" the presence of an absence comes into being. Death is precisely that absent presence. The prospect of one's own death is *in itself* an *immanent* element of non-integration.

Personally, I believe that when we are in contact with this absence, we register it as an *absence in our thinking*, which *never* allows us to achieve a stable level of integration. The bewilderment we feel vis-à-vis the mystery of our non-being remains an ineliminable and perturbing feature of our life, which undermines our capacity to achieve real integration, and leaves within us a feeling of incompleteness. I therefore believe that, in varying degrees, there is in all of us a constellation similar to the psychotic patients'. The very human predicament of never reaching a full integration coincides with the finite nature of our being. The very element demanding to be integrated, in reality, turns out to be an absence that prevents complete integration.

NOTES

(1) I would like to point out that in psychosis, delusions of persecution follow delusions of grandeur. Having satisfied the wish to eat from the tree of knowledge (wish to become God) induces guilt and is punished with persecution.

(2) If Searles' hypotheses were true, psychotic disturbances should occur later on in peoples' life. The most likely time should be the mid-life crisis, when the fear of old age and death become apparent to everyone.

12

AN UNTHINKABLE EVENT

> Navigare necesse est, vivere non necesse.
> (It is necessary to navigate, but not to live).
>
> Death, as a casket of nothingness, accommodates
> within itself what is essential to human beings.
> <div align="right">Martin Heidegger <i>Being and Time</i></div>

My reflection on the psychoanalytic approach to the question of death leads me to develop my own conceptualisations.

First of all, we need to re-frame Freud's statement that in the unconscious there is no representation of death, and consequently the fear of death, experienced on a conscious level, would have no bearing on the causation of suffering and psychopathology. The relationship between the unconscious and the awareness of death is a rather ambiguous one, however, and therefore it is not possible to think that we are not unconsciously frightened of death, solely because we are unable to perceive the ending of our life as individuals. Edgard Morin (1970) rightly pointed out that we are in danger of misunderstanding Freud's statement that human beings cannot believe in their own death, and therefore deep in their unconscious they are convinced that they are immortal. The denial of death to which Freud refers, does not coincide with the wish for immortality, present in religious thought. Religious creeds, in fact, acknowledging the reality of death on this earth, believe in a timeless afterlife. Indeed not to believe in one's own death and to believe in immortality are not the same thing. Freud does not talk so much about immortality, but rather about *a-mortality,* that is a sort of blindness with regard to the passing of time in one's life.

The most recent psychoanalytic theories describe the unconscious not only as the locus of omnipotent thinking, but also as the place of unconscious communication and truths, including the disagreeable ones, amongst which there is the idea of one's own death (De Masi, 2000). Moreover, multiple and contradictory beliefs co-exist in the unconscious. This is the reason why we are both oblivious and aware of our own death at the same time: we oscillate between an "internal time", which we would like to remain still and be repeatable, and an "external time", which flows only in one direction, is unrepeatable and moves irreversibly towards death. Death, however, continues to appear as something impossible, turned out to be real, yet felt to be a mistake, a punishment or a misfortune.

Human beings, unable to contemplate thoughts concerning death in their minds, resort to categories applicable to life, as, for instance the notion of *destiny.*

Sofsky (1996) writes:

> What is the foundation of our awareness of death? Death is not a life event. It is neither a finishing point nor a final agreement of settlement, but rather the exact opposite. We cannot live through our own death, nor can we experience it. We cannot have the experience of nothingness.

An event might be unthinkable, and still be unmistakably real: actually, as we know, what is not thinkable or representable is a greater source of anxiety and terror. Besides, how can we symbolise nothingness, that absent presence that death reveals itself to be? How can we mourn our own death, when the work of mourning can only occur in the presence of an absence, which was once a presence? What I would like to emphasise is that, inasmuch as it is extraneous to the symbolic order, our death as individuals is an experience of separation unlike any other form of mourning and therefore it triggers a specific anxiety, which cannot be worked through easily or assimilated to other partings. Rather, I would go as far as saying that, given the characteristics of our mental apparatus, the prospect of death is the *traumatic event* par excellence.

Freud (1920) employs the term trauma in a descriptive sense, imagining the human mind as enveloped within a kind of protective skin, which functions as a barrier against excessive stimuli and can also be perforated and lacerated by a wound. Offering protection against an excess of stimuli, selecting not only their quantity, but also their quality, is an essential function of the psychic apparatus. Babies and small children need their mothers to function as a protective shield, on the basis of their spontaneous capacity to understand intuitively what the infant can bear at different times, according to his or her emotional development. The mother acts as a protective screen, removing from the baby excessive and intolerable experiences.

Those adults who achieve an adequate mental development have internalised this maternal function, which they use consciously and unconsciously to protect themselves from anxiety. Naturally the level of anxiety tolerance varies from person to person. If it is too low, massive psychic defences, primarily splitting and denial, are employed and gradually this results in an amputation of that part of the personality, which exerts receptive and emotional functions. These excessive defences prevent people from interacting constructively with the rest of the world, and the inevitable effect is social isolation. However, even when there is a good selective capacity, at times there are events that could shatter every self-protective defence and throw even the most contained individual into a state of bewilderment and panic. One of these traumatic events, the most frightening of all, is certainly the terror of death (1), which can break through the protective membrane mentioned by Freud. In the face of death, in fact, our well established way of life disintegrates, our firmly held belief turns out to be a mere illusion and our useful defensive organisation, suddenly, is no longer available. Such an organisation, which we need in order to consolidate our life, is predicated upon the absence of the thought of death. When this veil tears, our belief in the world disappears. Who can protect us then? Who can decide our destiny? The trauma ensuing from the inevitability of death destroys the positive illusion that we can control our life. As a consequence, the deep-seated annihilation anxieties, which we all carry within ourselves, re-emerge. The equivalence between catastrophic trauma and death helps us to understand how much human beings need to obliterate the notion of death, and this necessity is what Freud so vehemently emphasises. The perception of death needs to be split off, because it constitutes an excessive trauma for our mind. Freud's statement that there is no idea of death in the unconscious perhaps means that we are not able to think about death in our unconscious mind, as we are not endowed with a suitable thinking potential to contemplate this thought.

The psychoanalysts who work with severely traumatised patients know what a complex task it is to transform the impact of the trauma on the mind. The catastrophe, having damaged the person's sense of self, leaves behind a thorough devastation, which prevents him or her from working through the trauma. For years, if not decades or even all throughout their lives, survivors cannot return to the places where they have been helpless victims of cruelty, where atrocious crimes have been committed, or they have been powerless witnesses of events that have destroyed their environment, their homes or killed their loved ones. After the trauma, survivors sever every connection with the traumatic experience, for fear that it might bring it back and any association with it might, once more, overwhelm them with the catastrophic terror, which destroyed every possible means of making sense of the event. Death is an equally devastating and meaningless trauma.

Freud (1925) differentiates anxiety experienced as a *real danger*, which he describes as automatic anxiety, from signal anxiety, activated vis-à-vis a *possible danger*. Signal anxiety warns us of a possible imminent danger and prepares us for that eventuality. As Caroline Garland claims (1998b), this distinction works well for the best part of our life, but after a traumatic occurrence, the ego is no longer able to differentiate signal from automatic anxiety. I believe that coming into contact with the thought of one's own death evokes a dread similar to traumatic anxiety where, in agreement with Freud, I would claim that danger signal coincides with automatic anxiety. (2) This is why the fear of death, a traumatic anxiety par excellence, is unthinkable and has to be denied. Nevertheless, it remains alive in our memory and can never be forgotten.

To be able to forget an experience, we need to work through, transform and digest it with our thinking apparatus. We can forget only what we can *digest*, just like dreams, whose function is to integrate our thoughts and this is why they are forgotten. Death is an *indigestible object*, laden with traumatic anxiety, like delusion or psychosis. This anxiety, albeit latent, is there all the time: the threat of a trauma to the self is like a fire under the ashes, which could be rekindled and reactivated by any association, memory or allusion. For this reason we are careful not to talk about it in public or remind our loved ones of it.

Psychic trauma and fear of death thus represent an unbearable rupture of the membrane which protects our life and whose roots are buried deeply into the unfathomable mystery of our body. Therefore the potentially traumatic fear of death needs to be denied as soon as we become aware of it and can never be "forgotten".

Recent psychoanalytic studies (Davies, 1996), corroborated by concordant neuroscientific discoveries (Le Doux, 1996), claim that our brain encodes traumatic memories in different ways from the ordinary ones. (3) Very frightening experiences stimulate mechanisms that inhibit explicit memory processes, causing a blockage of the capacity to recall these memories. In these cases, the defence mechanism employed to protect oneself from excessively painful or anxiety provoking events is *dissociation*. This radical defensive process separates traumatic experiences from the rest of the psyche, thus allowing the victim to function *as if* the trauma had never happened. Dissociation is "the only escape when there is no escape". This defence, necessary to the victim's mental survival at the time of the trauma, in the long run, produces alterations of his or her psychic functions, thus compromising the sense of personal integrity and continuity of life. The defence of dissociation prevents people from working through their trauma, by inhibiting their awareness of what has occurred and their memory recall. In reality, the perception of our own death remains *dissociated from* our awareness all throughout life.

Bion (1962) described the psychoanalytic experience as a field in which transformations occur and the same vicissitudes that accompany the infant's emotional development are replicated. In particular, the analyst helps the patient to transform what is intolerable into something that can be thought about. The therapist, with his or her capacity to intuitively imagine and contain painful experiences, should enable the patient to face his or her anxiety, instead of merely reacting to the trauma as something disruptive, liable to cause a breakdown of the capacity to think. This process, which can be more easily described than put into practice, would allow the patient to contemplate the thought of his or her own death, in the conscious awareness of the transience of life, thus achieving what, for Searles, was one of the aims of analysis.

From what I have been saying so far, it is clear that this transformation is particularly difficult, because of the traumatic quality of the fear of death. Those who work with severely traumatised persons know what profound transformations their traumas have produced in their psyche. The traumatic event has exposed the patient to the concrete experience of death, by suddenly facing him or her with a "nameless dread", arousing that annihilation anxiety, whose biological impact, even more than the psychological effects can de-structure the mind. The trauma produces a particularly destabilising effect when it is experienced alone and in a state of utter helplessness. Later difficulty in working through the trauma and the attendant panic are linked to the flashbacks, in particular to the sudden and intrusive sensation that the event is occurring in the present, rather than being remembered.

Normally we can remember an event without the sensation that we are re-living it, vivid as the memory might be. On the contrary, as a result of the de-structuring effect of the trauma, the distinction between the "I" and the event is lost and so the individual, without that necessary distance, is overwhelmed by a nameless dread. Remembering the events or mentally going over them is no longer possible, because a concrete re-living them has taken over. If the survivor hears certain words, which he or she associatively links with the traumatic event, the trauma is very literally brought back again and again.

My hypothesis is that for all of us the occurrence of death is a real trauma, not really experienced in the past, but projected into the future, which can provoke the same sudden and intrusive sensation that we are re-living the overwhelming event, rather than just thinking about it. For this reason we try to eliminate from our usual vocabulary any word which might function as a stimulus to associations with death, and this results in a permanent dissociation of the latter from our consciousness. The surprising lack of symbolic meanings and the concreteness of our thinking regarding death are evidence of the existence of an area of helplessness in our mind vis-à-vis this event.

I believe that Freud refers to the *dissociation* ensuing from a traumatic experience, when he talks about the *denial of death* in our unconscious. It is well known, in fact, that Freud solves the problem of death, felt to be an intolerable trauma, claiming that consciously we are aware of our transience, whilst unconsciously we deny it. According to Freud, the proof of the absence of death in the unconscious is given by our inclination to represent our own death as if we were still alive. Human beings tend to observe themselves as alive and entertaining a dialogue with themselves and others, while they imagine themselves as dead. In reality when people reflect on death, they cannot but be alive and, consequently, their fantasies can never disregard the experience of the continuity of life.

Are human creatures, who cannot know their own death for ontological reasons, able to resort to any known and familiar experiences, to be able to represent it? I think that, when people represent death as a continuation of life, they inevitably end up regarding it as the most painful of human sufferings. When we imagine being dead, we think of ourselves as alive, but extremely alone and separated from the rest of all the other living creatures.

In the previous pages, I pointed out that *the unconscious representation of death is similar to the psychotics' representation of their mental state*. In fact, psychotic patients, in spite of their awareness of being alive, perceive themselves as dead and separate from the world, which they have abandoned and which has lost meaning for them. (4) When death is represented in the unconscious, it appears as a timeless agony, an unending life permeated by the painful feeling of being dead. Human beings represent death as utter isolation and timeless segregation. This is why I believe that Freud was right when he claimed that *real death* is absent in the unconscious. I also think, however, that Melanie Klein was equally astute when she detected the presence of *another death* that is precisely *psychic death*: the feeling of being alive, but in a paralysed condition. Moreover, her theory of destructiveness and envy led her to link the fear of death to psychic suffering and psychopathology.

If, in the course of our life, we achieve a precarious equilibrium, based on the idealisation of our sense of self, with the arrival of old age, anticipating the inevitable end of our days, we begin to feel hatred towards life for abandoning us, and so our envy for those who will survive us is strengthened. In this context, death is inevitably perceived as persecution and suffering. On the other hand, our clinical experience shows time and time again how, if the good internal object is absent, the fear of death is fought against with the very same derivatives of the death instinct: pathological narcissism, addictive defences and various forms of perverse sexuality. These defences, in turn, create a vicious circle, and in so doing they intensify the anxieties the person wanted to allay in the first place. The fear of death, already present in all of us, in these cases becomes more intense. Indeed, when they have to face the inevitable end of their life, these patients' awareness that they have irreparably destroyed vital parts of themselves arouses further persecutory feelings. The conflict between constructiveness and destructiveness, truth and falseness, omnipotent illusion and reality goes on all throughout life.

In conclusion, to think about our own death consists in facing the ultimate encounter with ourselves, knowing the reality of our life and its authenticity, at a time when we can no longer evade the truth. When the derivatives of the death instinct dominate, such as envy, greed and unconscious falseness, sooner or later, the person's pathological structures are strained and a cruel and implacable super-ego will persecute the "sinner" mercilessly. This unconscious fantasy of a harsh and implacable judge is corroborated by the religious belief in God's last judgement awaiting human beings after they die.

NOTES

(1) Only in extremes cases of perceptive perversions, like the one I have described in chapter 4, can death be unconsciously desired and pursued triumphantly. Even in these cases, however, we can wonder whether the child

might have been exposed too early to emotional and environmental traumas that prevented the constitution of an effectively protective psychic shield.

(2) However, we can also find the same configuration in some other forms of psychopathology. If someone suffered from delusions of persecution, in the course of which they felt their life to be in danger, when they come out of their delusion, they still carry within the delusional traumatic anxiety. Thus any associative element, memory, word or object, even remotely linked to the psychotic episode, could precipitate the delusional anxiety to re-surface. Similar considerations apply to phobia, which I have talked about in chapter 3.

(3) Le Doux (1996), a well-known neuroscientist, says, "Unconscious memories of fear, established through the amygdala, seem to be branded in the brain".

(4) Abadi (1984), albeit in different ways, links representation of death and psychosis: "Death, as a disintegration and dissolution of the personality, finds its expression in madness. Madness is a way of representing death to ourselves. If life is the result of a particular relationship of the subject, endowed with a body, with the world, death or the cessation of life can come about through the annihilation of the subject or the world. Thus madness becomes a representation of death, inasmuch as it involves the destruction of the two terms whose interaction we call life".

13

DEATH: WHAT REPARATION?

Neither my birth nor my death can
feel as my own experiences.
Maurice Merleau-Ponty

It is natural to die as to be born; and to a little infant,
perhaps the one is as painful as the other.
Francis Bacon, *Essay on Death*

When constructive aspects prevail in people's psyche, they endeavour, more or less consciously, to give their lives a coherent and systematic shape, from which they can derive a sense of identity and meaning.

According to Alberto Spagnoli (1995), in old age it is possible to achieve a balance between despair and acceptance by means of a reappraisal of the past, which leads to a new equilibrium, without grudge or too many regrets. It is possible to come through a state of despair by accepting responsibility, developing a capacity to mourn what is lost and becoming aware that what has been done can no longer be changed. This integration needs to be built on very solid bases, if it is to withstand the thought of death, which is a negation of life, a threat to stability and a constant challenge to the meaning of human existence. We can counter this inevitable drive towards nothingness only when we create an experience of constructive order, which can make sense of and give meaning to our life. In so doing, we can mitigate the pain of loss and take leave from a valuable and useful life, without too much despair. At the time when we can no longer turn away from the thought of our transience, the pain for what we lose, the intensity of the rage and envy we feel towards those who remain, can be mitigated through a capacity to tolerate our aloneness and the encounter with other human beings. (1)

The capacity to be alone and not feel isolated is largely linked to a sense of continuity and personal meaning in the face of the object's absence, in other words I am referring to the negative capability of memory. The greater this capacity appears to be, the more we have had positive experiences, which have gathered and reside in our emotional world and continue to animate it. To be able to develop what Klein and Winnicott define as the *capacity to be alone*, we need to have experienced an acknowledgement of our separate identity through our caregivers' love. This recognition lays the foundation for a capacity to love and give, with pleasure, to our objects more than we expect from them. The capacity to be alone is predicated upon the achievement of personal integration, which is the prerequisite to be able to tolerate our finite nature, without too much resentment. After all, life, as well as any other object, cannot always be within our possession: we should be able to allow life, too, to take leave from us.

In what way can a personal analysis help us deal with the issue of our finite nature?

Since *Analysis Terminable and Interminable,* analysts have wondered about the length of psychoanalytic treatments and have reflected upon the maturational effects of the experience of separation. Thinking about the possible ending of a treatment, the analyst wonders what sort of psychic equipment the patient has been able to build in the course of the therapy, to deal successfully with whatever experiences life might still have in store for him or her. (2) Once an agreement on a termination date has been reached, the last phase of the analysis can prove to be very rewarding. The wish to go over the changes and consolidate them, the need to process the anxiety for the impending separation, the necessity to keep the analysis alive and to be kept in the analyst's mind are experiences that contribute to and strengthen the process of integration.

Out of all the experiences characterising the ending of an analysis, what deserves a special attention is the perception of time, which, at this point, has a definite limit and cannot therefore be considered as endless. In spite of the knowledge of the imminent ending, both the analysand and the analyst need to maintain alive the experience of their relationship that does not disappear, solely because they will part, but remains significant until the very last minute. This dual perception of time, which flows and is experienced, at the same time, helps the analysand to develop the capacity to tolerate the transience of life, that very secret which Freud would have liked to be able to transmit to the melancholic poet, unable to appreciate the beauty of nature, as it is doomed to wither.

It is necessary, however, to differentiate the psychological experience of separation and mourning from death proper, because the impact of these two events on our mind occurs on different levels. A good enough experience of separation develops the patient's capacity to keep the relationship with the analyst alive in the internal world, thus offering some comfort for the loss of the real object. When two people have had a mutually significant relationship, they do not lose their emotional capacity to remember it, after they have parted. (3) I therefore believe that, if on the hand an analysis well conducted and focused on the work of mourning helps us to think about the finiteness of our life, on the other hand, it cannot dispel, for analysand and analyst alike, the anxiety concomitant with the thought that we go through death utterly alone. Whilst a separation can potentially be integrated, the same cannot be said about the experience of one's own death. Death, in fact, which entails the destruction of our symbolic and emotional world as our only means to work through the loss, at the same time eludes the work of mourning and transforms the loss into a nameless dread. I hold the view that the psychoanalytic journey allows the patient to re-find the meaning of life and accept its mystery and finiteness, yet it cannot offer any comfort for the lack of future and the destruction of the potential self, implicit in the prospect of death. At this point, we encounter the ultimate limit of every human endeavour, including psychoanalysis. We need to accept that the therapeutic process, which permits the mobilisation of the reparative processes, finds here its limit. Reparation, in fact, can occur only when it is possible to imagine ourselves projected into the future. The definite obliteration of time associated to the representation of death makes it impossible to regard reparation as a way of working through the anxiety for the destruction of the self.

Bauman (1992) points out that the basic awareness of human mortality accounts for many crucial aspects of the social and cultural organisation of highly developed societies. We can understand many, if not all the societies known to us, better, or rather in a new way, if we conceptualise them as different ways of facing the knowledge of death, by transforming it from an impossible predicament into a primary source of meaning of life. From this perspective, human beings' ceaseless efforts to build their civilisations would represent an inalienable attempt to make reparation in the face of the danger of death. (4)

Paradoxically, then, the awareness and fear of death, whose presence is a constant factor in human creatures' experiences, would constitute an alarm signal inscribed in our being, in order to strengthen our attachment to life and project it into the future. Through the creation of shared myths, which found the social group's identity and history and permit its projection into the future, the fear of death appears to achieve a certain equilibrium. Whilst this is undoubtedly true for the group, the individual does not find an easy solution to the fear of death.

Aware as we are of our transience, we know that we will die whilst others will go on living, will expand their knowledge and look at the world of the future, whereas we will not be able to. Renouncing the fantasy of immortality should not lead to the destruction of every *illusion* and hope in what is still possible. As Karl Jaspers states, the thirst for eternity that inspires human beings does have a profound meaning. As we have an enduring need to extend our life into the future, and likewise to expand our potential knowledge of the world, then it is necessary and vital to preserve the role of illusion, for as long as we live. The desire for immortality needs to be transformed into hope for what is still possible. Such hope, preserved until the end, is a gift to others, as well.

We go through life accompanied by our uncertainty and ignorance of all its possibilities, holding onto the necessary co-existence of illusions and personal myths, which structure our psychic reality, in the world of our imagination. We achieve integration by becoming aware of these structures, rather than by destroying them. The capacity to think, that pervades our life, originates from our imagination and its ability to project into the future. (5) To be able to think, we need to be able to use our imagination.

In play and pretend games, children feel free to create, on the strength of their knowledge that they are exploring a different reality, which does not belong to them and they cannot know or fully understand yet, as they can only sense its existence. They employ their imagination to create a reality not lived yet, but inhabited by others. "Let's pretend that I am . . ." indicates the fantasy area necessary for psychic development. Play, understood as make-believe, a habitual and predominant activity in infancy, remains a constant feature until a certain age and later is gradually replaced by other imaginative activities, like, for instance, love or falling in love, fighting for one's ideals or religious faith. Religion itself belongs to the realm of imagination and one of its functions resides in its capacity to provide a space open to life and hope. Moreover, its strength is located precisely in its provision of a shared area of illusion. Also it powerfully unites or divides groups, giving them a common identity. Most importantly, it is an open space, similar to children's play, where there is a place for belief, as much as for doubt. No believer is fully convinced of the whole reality of the religious universe where he or she belongs. The activity of our imagination, then, similar to our capacity to dream, should never die out, if we want our psychic life to continue. I believe that psychosis or psychic death is the inevitable destiny ensuing from the destruction of imagination.

Whether our thirst for life, immanent to our thinking, coalesces into an individual fantasy (the unconscious cannot believe in its own death) or a philosophical perspective, or a shared creation of myths and religions, this belief, nonetheless, constitutes an irreducible nucleus whose essential task is to process the permanently threatening thought of death. For this reason the analyst goes on working up until the last session and until the very last minute of the analysis. The analysand, in turn, contributes to the mental growth of the analyst.

As they age, people turn back to look at their past and wonder what they have achieved. If their past has been meaningful, it is easier to preserve the hope of being kept alive in the minds of those who will survive and be remembered for whatever good they have been able to do. This, however, is not enough to come to terms with the end of life. The inescapable contrast between the finiteness of our body and the incommensurable development of our mind brings back all the time the insoluble conflict between the desire to live and the prospect of death, felt to be the ultimate annihilation of our potentially infinite subjectivity. It is, therefore, a necessary feature of life to confront the reality of our dissolution and lack of future. When we can no longer elude the awareness of our transience, we need to be able to project the inexhaustible potential of our being into objects different from us. At this point, it is important to have close real objects who can contain the projections of our potential selves, like children, friends, pupils, institutions or the human values which we have loved and struggled for. If these objects are not available, because we have destroyed them internally or have been unable to create them, then we really experience death as a tragedy. In this instance, our self, with its unremitting aspiration to continuity, precipitates and gets lost in an empty space, filled with nameless dread. Schizophrenics experience the same anxiety, as they have severed all their ties to the world, destroyed their symbolic universe and consequently cannot project into their objects. If the fear of death is equivalent to the catastrophic occurrence of psychosis, the self, in order to be safe, needs to be able to imagine carrying on its existence in others who will go on living.

The real tragedy, unthinkable and beyond every possible reparation, is not so much the death of the individual self, but the destruction of humanity and the universe which has given us a home and allows us to experience a sense of continuity; the irreparable damage is the total destruction of the world and its future memory.

The secret of our well being, thus, resides in our capacity to go on nurturing our reasons for being constructive and alive, against the forces of inertia, disintegration and anxiety. Therefore, the destruction of the structures of our communal living, instrumental to re-create the whole of society in its unforeseeable potentiality, turns out to be as blameworthy as the annihilation of the inner protections, which we deploy to guarantee our physical and psychic life. From this perspective, we can understand how living under the terrorist domination of the fear of death, internalised as a bad object, represents not only a danger, but a fault as well.

As we go through the aging process, the richness of the experiences we have assimilated through having been children, adults and finally old, appears incomparable to the narrowness of our future. If, on the one hand, the possibility of our future expansion decreases, on the other, we identify ever more with our past, which appears as the expanded time of our life. Being able to rethink our past in the light of the experiences, which we have acquired, is an aspect of the constructive work we can do, to allow ourselves to live creatively the last part of our life. This is the wisdom of old people. Coming to terms with the inevitability of death and accepting the disappearance of our individual self goes hand in hand with the integration of the past, and this psychic work promotes our mental growth until the end of our days. This continuous integration of the past becomes even more meaningful the more we are able to accept the mystery of our transience. An integrated sense of self gives us a measure of safety, which is essential to be able to project into the future of others and, in so doing, avoid the catastrophic sense of dissolution into nothingness. If we are unable to work through the pain of the disappearance of our individual self, projecting into others would represent merely an idealising defence in the service of our narcissistic desire to go on living.

When we face death and attempt to leave behind our own self, we can only find solace in collective, rather than individual reparation. Even when we go through the process of dying, in itself a lonely journey, paradoxically, we still need the presence of others. In the face of death, reparation consists in the arduous journey of many individual selves who leave themselves in other selves that will follow. Reparation can only be achieved *through the past*, through the projection of our past into the future, *in the future of others*.

NOTES

(1) A representation of the intense suffering of the dying person caused by his envy for those who remain is contained in Arthur Schnitzler's story *Dying* (1892).

(2) In most cases, having thought about it, patient and analyst agree on a termination date. In some cases, instead, we are faced by the analysand's anxious refusal to end the analysis. This could be seen as one of those instances of psychoanalytic "claustrophilia", to borrow Elvio Fachinelli's (1983) definition. This wish to remain forever in the psychoanalytic claustrum, fantasying a timeless analysis, seems to be not only a defence against any new experience, but also against the awareness of human transience.

(3) I am obviously describing a favourable situation, but in reality the work of mourning is very complex and yields uncertain results. In fact it is always possible that new traumatic events occur and shake the previously reached equilibrium.

(4) In Greek thought, for instance, nature is immortal, as it exists independently of both the Gods and human beings. Only human creatures are mortal and so are all their artefacts, their works, facts and words. Only through narration, human events are rescued from mortality and oblivion, to be handed down to posterity. In the great Greek tragic and epic myths, transmitted for centuries through oral narration, the deification of warriors and heroes has precisely the meaning of creating a permanent tradition. Excellence (*aretè*) is what justifies the narration of history. In Greek culture, after the mythical-poetic phase, the sense of excellence could be achieved only within the human community: the *polis*, where maintaining the political ties and participating to public life become the supreme aim in life and the supreme goodness. I draw these thoughts from Hannah Arendt's essay "Active Life", as Giovanna Bettini summarises them in the preface to *Ebraismo e modernità* (Feltrinelli, Milan 1993) by the same author.

(5) As Freud (1911) had written in "Formulations on the two Principles of Mental Functioning", the pleasure principle, which predates the reality principle, carries on working after the establishment of the latter and thus represents a mode of thinking, which works in parallel with the reality principle.

PART TWO

The unconscious and death in Freud and in Melanie Klein

14

THE DENIAL OF DEATH

Therefore the most distressing of our woes, death,
is nothing for us, because when we are present, death is not
and when death is present, then we are not.
Thus death is nothing for the living, it is nothing for
the dead, because in the former it does not exist, the
latter are no more.
Epicurus, Letter to Mycenaean

We learn how to die all throughout our life.
Seneca, Letter to Lucilius

Freud comes to reflect explicitly on the themes of separation, mourning and death relatively late. Only after his description of the impact of sexuality on the child's mind, does he deal with these big themes. Perhaps the First World War, with its grief, victims and destruction of the social institutions might have increased his sensitivity to this theme, as proven by the chronology of his writings on this topic. In the initial phases of the conflict, Freud let himself be carried away with naive patriotic optimism. Soon, however, he moves onto a phase of reappraisal, which produces his works on the question of war and death. The conference entitled "Death and Us", for the Jewish Association

B'nai B'rith was held in 1915 and "Thoughts for the Times on War and Death" was written in the same year.

Already in January, Freud announces a few of these themes that were preoccupying him, in a letter to the Dutch psychiatrist Frederik van Eeden. Our intellect, he writes, is something very fragile, dependent on instincts and affects; human beings' primitive and evil impulses have not at all disappeared, and go on living in the unconscious of all of us, albeit in a state of repression. In the present war, so-called "civilised" nations are responsible for unimaginable cruelties and injustice, and they fight each other with evident bad faith.

In the conference held some time later for the Jewish Association, Freud emphasises that human beings cannot bear to hear about death, actually they would rather "bury it in silence". For most, death seems to come about by chance, rather than by necessity. When a loved one dies, in fact, it is natural to think that the danger could have been recognised earlier, so as to prevent death. Even when death comes as a result of collective calamity, as in the case of war, people stubbornly regard it as an extraordinary event. War, adds Freud, changes the perception of death, which no longer appears to be the product of chance, but is, instead, daily and really present with its victims. The obvious insecurity of human existence, paradoxically, restores the value and meaning of life.

In "Thoughts for the Times on War and Death" Freud talks about war as an event that shatters all the familiar barriers, ignores the prerogatives of injured and doctors alike, makes no differentiation between those who fight and those who do not, violates property rights and destroys with its blind fury all that it finds in its way. When men are at war, they behave as if they would never return to a peaceful future life. War wipes out any illusion regarding the goodness of human creatures and shows how, in reality, they have never emancipated themselves from their primitive status. It is inevitable to think that the State bars the individual from using violence, not so much because it intends to suppress it, but only because it wishes to monopolise it for its own sake. Injustice and violence, which dishonour an individual, are legitimatised by a collectively recourse to them. The destructiveness of war brings to the fore the problem of death, which cannot be repudiated or seen as an exceptional occurrence.

Freud states that the individual cannot represent death. Nobody believes in his or her death, and in our unconscious we all firmly believe in our immortality. Every time we try to think of ourselves as dead, we cannot but see ourselves as spectators through the eyes of those who observe us. If death is not representable, we cannot experience it elsewhere but in our imagination: we die in identification with the hero, yet we also survive him.

In front of someone dead, we adopt a very particular attitude; we show admiration, abstain from criticism, and forgive every possible fault: *de mortuis nihil nisi bonum* (about the dead we cannot say but good things). Respect for the dead, who no longer need it, becomes more important than respect for the truth and, in some cases, even than respect for the living. This formal respect disappears in the case of a loved one; in this instance death has an enormous power over the life of the surviving person, whose existence seems to become impoverished and meaningless.

The primordial history of humanity is made out of endless murders. Primitive beings were ruthless in their capacity to cause their neighbours' death; they felt radically differently about other people's death and their own. For them, killing was the obvious thing to do. War seems to bring back the most primitive organisation in relation to death: it presents foreigners as enemies to be eliminated, and pushes people to become heroes who deny the reality of their mortality. If it is true that primitive people kill their enemies and deny the possibility of their own death, yet, when someone else dies, they have to acknowledge that it might happen to them, even though they deny it at the same time.

Thinking about the feelings aroused by the sight of the dead body of the loved ones, says Freud, we can trace the origin not only of the doctrine of the soul and the belief in immortality, but also of the earliest moral commandments. Witnessing the deterioration of the corpse creates a distinction between a body and a soul and consolidates the belief in other forms of existence and in an after-life, on the basis of the persisting memory of the deceased. So becomes possible the imagining of previous lives, transmigration and reincarnations of souls; all this with the aim of removing from death its meaning as the final annihilation of life.

"Thou shall not kill" is the reversal of the original aggressive position: the imperative not to kill gradually begins to include unfamiliar and unloved strangers and, lastly, enemies as well. Unable to acknowledge the presence of what is disadvantageous, the unconscious adopts, before death, the same attitude as primitive people: it cannot conceive of death, but can only attribute to it a negative content. Therefore, if death is not susceptible of psychoanalytic investigation, it is better to focus our enquiry on human beings' unconscious attitude vis-à-vis death. This choice offers, at least, the advantage of allowing a greater sincerity as well as making our life, perhaps, more bearable. Recalling the old adage: *si vis pacem, para bellum* (if you want peace, get ready for war), Freud suggests changing it into: *si vis vitam, para mortem* (if you want to be alive, get ready for death).

15

THE PROBLEM OF MOURNING

We do not hear when the divine melody is
whispered, we hear only when it is silent.

> Hans Carossa

When we fall, I believe it will be for good,
and we will not be able to get up again like
actors murdered on stage.

> Jean Rostand

The grief for the loss of a beloved person or for the separation from our love objects, which is associated to the thought of death, cannot easily be differentiated. In his 1915 paper "Mourning and Melancholia" Freud explains the dynamics of pathological mourning, which leads to melancholia. As we have pointed out describing Rilke's state of mind, melancholia expresses the pain that reveals an unconscious conflict between the person who feels abandoned and the abandoning love object. After the loss, the melancholic feels that life has become meaningless and his or her own ego is empty. Those who experience grief accuse their lost object of betrayal and therefore, unconsciously, hate it. The hatred is directed not only against the abandoning object, but also against the ego itself, which is then devalued and attacked. In reality the attacks against the ego are directed at the object. The melancholic's bond with the object prevents any resolution of the love/hate relationship with the loved person, as in the case of the poet reproaching nature for being ephemeral and inconsistent. The pain for the loss, seemingly stronger than love, does not allow the grief to be worked through and acceptance of the reality of the separation.

With regard to depressive illnesses, like melancholia, the clinical picture is clearer than in a normal process of mourning. In the latter we do not understand so well why the process is so lengthy or what its vicissitudes might be. To explain the difficulty in accepting separation, Freud reminds us of the stickiness of the libido, which binds us to our love objects. Once the loss has occurred, the libido refuses to renounce the object, not even when its substitute is there, already available.

Karl Abraham worked with Freud on the theme of depression and mourning, but he was able to go further. What happens, Abraham asks himself (1924), when the ordinary work of mourning is successful? What processes do we normally employ to work through the loss and eventually succeed in detaching ourselves from the lost object? Abraham puts forward the hypothesis that getting over normal grief occurs through a process of internal reparation, that is, through the *psychic* reconstruction of the lost object inside the ego. The work of mourning would thus consist in the possibility of a stable re-introjection of the image and the memory of the loved object within one's inner world. This is the only means whereby the lost object, having re-established itself in the ego, can be re-animated and experienced as still alive. The internalisation of the lost object in the psychic world is a compensation for the real loss and it also facilitates the working through of the pain and the depressive emptiness. Abraham illustrates this process, talking about a patient who, having recently lost his wife, dreams that the individual and detached parts of her body reunite, and the woman begins to give new signs of life. The scene calls to mind a butcher's shop where animals' body parts are exposed, and therefore it conveys a funereal atmosphere. Yet, at the same time, the dream announces the success of the "work of mourning", whereby the loved object is no longer in a fragmented state or destroyed. The patient can revive it, restore its integrity and carry it inside as a lively object. According to Abraham, it is only the *introjection of the lost object of love within the internal world* that permits us to work through grief.

Whilst Freud emphasises how the libido needs to come to terms with the loss and find another love object, indicating that the gradual waning of the pain results from the pressure of reality, Abraham points out the importance of the introjection and psychic restoration of the lost object in the internal world. The essential difference between normal and pathological mourning, like melancholia, is that in the latter the *process of reanimation,* which is the foundation of the work of mourning, cannot take place because it is impeded by unconscious hatred. The depressed person internalises a love object within the frame of an aggressive tie that binds him or her indissolubly to the object. Between the ego and the object a strong sado-masochistic relationship is established, which prevents the reintrojection of the object in the internal world. Conversely, in ordinary grief this process is possible, because love allows the mourner to revive and reconstitute the internal object, overcoming the unconscious resentment for being abandoned. In essence, the work of mourning is completed when we can allow the loved person to part and leave us, preserving them as good within us. So we can go on appreciating internally, rather than reproaching them for the deprivation and loss inflicted on us or hating the entire world of human relationships. In conclusion, the work of mourning coincides with the capacity to allow the object to have a separate existence, renouncing any further claims or possession.

16

THE DEATH INSTINCT

> Death, dear Brutus, is not inscribed in
> the skies, but in ourselves.
> > William Shakespeare, *Julius Caesar*

> The utensils, which sculpt the face of
> cell life have, originally, perhaps
> the potential to sculpt the face of death.
> > Jean-Claude Ameisen, *At the Heart of Life*

In 1920, in *Beyond the Pleasure Principle*, Freud introduces some of his thoughts about death, which touch upon the very foundation of psychoanalytic theory, as he had previously formulated it. Alongside libido, the only instinct considered until then, he places the death instinct, as a representative of a biological force even more powerful than the life drive. The life instinct tends to modify or neutralise it, in vain, because the latter prevails in the end. The instinctual "correlation", that justifies the death instinct, would correspond to the human tendency to repeat unpleasurable experiences. This tendency to repeat negative events contradicts, according to Freud, the notion that people seek solely the satisfaction of their erotic drives, and indicates, instead, the existence and activity of a drive towards unpleasure and death, in the unconscious.

THE DEATH INSTINCT

The death instinct, however, cannot fully express itself, because it is amalgamated and fused with the libidinal drive. Only when a de-fusion occurs, does it manifest itself through unambiguous psychopathological states. Under normal circumstances, the death drive is subsumed by the aim of bringing the living organism back to a quiet state. In fact it works *silently* outside consciousness and beyond every possibility of being represented in the unconscious.

> If we can consider it as an experimental and absolutely certain fact, with no exceptions, that everything living dies for internal reasons –becomes inorganic once again – then we shall be compelled to say that 'the aim of all life is death' and, looking backwards, that 'inanimate things existed before living ones'.

This is a radically new perspective, but, at the same time, it does not contradict the previous statement, stressed several times, that the unconscious cannot contain a representation of death. Freud does not think that there might be a connection between the death instinct and the fear of death. The death instinct would relate to the genesis of primary masochism, repetition compulsion, resistance to recovery, but, as it is not representable, it would not generate anxiety and would not be linked to the experience of one's own death. Freud is very clear on this issue. To Stekel, who believes that every anxiety is linked to the fear of death, Freud replies that the fear of death is not directly linked to the perception of one's own death, but it has a different significance and different connections. Freud reiterates that the unconscious does not acknowledge the idea of death and holds onto the infantile belief in immortality. When death breaks through into consciousness, it always concerns someone else's death. (1) Hence, the reasons underlying neurotic suffering must come from something else:

> The fear of death presents a difficult problem to psychoanalysis, for death is an abstract concept with a negative content for which no unconscious correlative can be found. It would seem that the mechanism of the fear of death can

only be that the ego relinquishes its narcissistic libidinal cathexis in a very large measure (. . .) I believe that the fear of death is something that occurs between the ego and the super-ego (. . .) The fear of death in melancholia only admits of one explanation: that the ego gives itself up because it feels itself hated and persecuted by the super-ego, instead of loved. (Freud, 1923).

In 1926, he states:

But the unconscious seems to contain nothing that could give any content to our concept of the annihilation of life.

And a few lines further on, he writes:

But nothing resembling death can ever have been experienced; or if it has, as in fainting, it has left no observable traces behind. I am therefore inclined to adhere to the view that the fear of death should be regarded as analogous to the fear of castration . . .

Freud's conclusion seems to be that the fear of death, which looms over us more than we like to think, does not come from our perception of the immanence of death, but from our feeling of guilt, from castration anxiety or from the loss of the super-ego's love. Above all, Freud focuses on castration anxiety, which he regards as the prototype of all the anxieties, from the loss of the breast to the anxiety ensuing from trauma:

These considerations make it possible to regard the fear of death, like the fear of conscience, as a development of the fear of castration. (Freud, 1922)

Even in "Inhibitions Symptoms and Anxiety" (1926), the fear of death observable in clinical symptomatology is not taken at face value:

The unconscious seems to contain nothing that could give any content to our concept of the annihilation of life (. . .) nothing resembling death can ever have been experienced

THE DEATH INSTINCT

(. . .) I am therefore inclined to adhere to the view that the fear of death should be regarded as analogous to the fear of castration.

All his closest pupils defended these statements by Freud, in an intransigent manner, even though they appear to be unsustainable in many respects. For instance Fenichel (1946) claims:

It is questionable whether there is such thing as a normal fear of death; actually the idea of one's own death is subjectively inconceivable, and therefore probably every fear of death covers other unconscious ideas.

All Freudian analysts consider the unconscious as the locus of desire and libidinal satisfaction, and therefore it cannot contain a representation of death. (2)

Clearly Freud counters the awareness of death with the omnipotence of unconscious thinking. Moreover Freud claims that in the unconscious our life span is eternal and uninterrupted, as he seems more interested in emphasising the unconscious denial of death than in understanding its impact on life. The unconscious would thus behave as an Egyptian Pharaoh, engaged in a lifelong endeavour to build his immortality, because ancient Egyptians held the view that bodily decay and the cancellation of the name of the dead prevented their return to life. If the problem of death is not registered in the unconscious, it follows that the fear of death has no part to play in the aetiology of suffering and psychopathology.

In his conceptualisation of the unconscious Freud gradually shifts towards acknowledging anxiety. As he moves to the new structural model of the mind (1923), he leaves behind the notion that the sole aim of the unconscious is the fulfilment of pleasure or that anxiety always derives from unsatisfied desires, from an accumulation of libido that cannot be discharged. In 1926 he maintains that, when an event impacts traumatically on the psychic apparatus, its effect is the annihilation of the defences against anxiety. Even though the triggering element is external, the anxiety comes from internal sources. Freud lists five sources of anxiety, universal and traumatic for us all: birth, castration anxiety, loss of the loved object, loss of the object's love and annihilation anxiety. Nevertheless, even though listing the various types of anxiety, Freud refers explicitly to the separation from or the loss of something felt to be essential to one's life, he will never go as far as stating that human beings, inasmuch as they experience anxiety rather than deny it, can acknowledge the reality of death. According to Freud, in fact, the denial of death occurs anyway. Because of the ambivalence deeply woven into all our love relationships, we can perceive a negative event that strikes the other and spares us with a sense of triumph. This can happen when death strikes another person, someone close as well. Freud thought that we unconsciously experience our loved ones as rivals: they are dear to us, but they are also strangers.

Feeling relieved, or even triumphant for having being spared has important consequences for those who survive traumatic events in which other people have lost their lives, including relatives and close friends. In addition to the impact of the traumatic experience, they have to deal with the onerous task of mourning the loss of those who did not survive. Paradoxically, in those circumstances, their survival is felt to be yet another traumatic experience, because their survivor guilt increases the burden of the pain for what is lost.

I believe that the guilt for having being spared, which is an important component of the intense suffering of survivors of traumas or great collective tragedies, is also an aspect of the grief ensuing from the loss of someone close. An important feature of the work of mourning, besides the anger towards the abandoning object, which Freud and Abraham pointed out, is precisely the feeling of guilt for one's survival, which is not sufficiently emphasised. The latter are depressive pain and guilt and do not derive from the disappointment the survivor feels for the abandonment, but rather from his or her fantasy of the dead person's suffering. This guilt can reach such intensity that it spoils the survivor's life. The identification with the dead person and his or her suffering leads to grief and melancholia. Paradoxically, feeling dead in identification with the dead object seems preferable to feeling alive and having to bear the pain of the guilt for having survived. (3)

Only a close reading of Freud's works on mourning and war, which emphasises their relation to his later theory of the death instinct, does reveal the full richness of his contribution to the understanding of the psychological meaning of our transience. With his emphasis on the need to tolerate the thought of loss and to work through grief, Freud tells us that, if life consists in the capacity to think about death, whilst appreciating, at the same time, the time we do have, then it is necessary to work through the pain caused by the awareness of our transience, all the time.

The psychotherapist Adam Phillips (1999) seems to capture very clearly this aspect of the death instinct, as a force within us. This means, according to Phillips, that, constitutionally, we are all suicide, not so much out of despair, but because dying is, literally, within our nature

In Freud's thought, death is both a paradoxical and exemplary wish. The need for redemption, which is an essential characteristic of every theology, lays its foundation in our feelings of inadequacy, in this world. Without a God who might remember us, we are and feel impoverished and transient. In many religions death is seen as a sin or a punishment, and this idea is associated with the ultimate humiliation. On the contrary, the hypothesis of the death instinct tells us that, even when we renounce our illusion of immortality, we are not diminished by our transience.

Phillips thinks that Freud is fascinated by the losses that we do successfully survive: this positive view of loss is often a recurrent theme in Freud's writings. But what kind of loss does death entail? When Freud introduces the theory of the death instinct, one of his aims is to make death bearable and coherent within a secular framework. This compels us to ascertain whether the word "loss" is, in this case, still correct. Our feeling diminished or frightened by the passing of time indicates that we have not been able to think. Even a very young child, immersed in the cotton reel game (*Beyond the Pleasure Principle*, 1920), which he makes appear and disappear, thus re-living the drama of the object's loss and the mother's absence, learns that loss is a constant feature of life.

According to Freud, the human challenge consists in the capacity to process this loss, without despair, but also without a flight into optimism and omnipotence. Freud, claims Phillips, maintains that we can develop a capacity to leave behind our attachment to people and to ourselves, as well. The biggest problem resides in the difficulty in separating from our irresistible wish for immortality and desire for permanence. Therefore we need to give up our notion of timeless ideals and yearnings for eternity. Phillips points out that Freud taught us that life is more extraordinary than death and, paradoxically, we can grasp more faithfully the mystery of life when we observe the presence of the death instinct. Our only life derives from the existence of our bodily ego and death is part of life, whatever form it might take. All considered, Freud wishes us to be not too frightened of our mortality, bur rather to live with the thought of death.

Freud's death, as it occurred in reality, and has been narrated by those who witnessed it, is an impressive confirmation of his reflections. He met his destiny free from desires or illusions: addressing his physician, doctor Schur, to remind him of their "agreement" not to abandon him in the imminence of death and to help him die, Freud asked him to tell his daughter Anna that the time had come.

> Freud's readings were not without significance; he chose his books with great care. The last book he read was *The Wild Ass' Skin* by Balzac. When he finished reading it, he told me, as if by chance: "It was the right book for me to read, it talks about shrivelling and starvation."(4)

It is astonishing how the existence of the death instinct has recently received validation by modern biological studies, which seem to echo Freud's intuition, when he states that the aim of what is alive is death and that every living being dies for *internal* reasons. In order to account for the self-destruction of the cells, after they have accomplished their biological task, modern biology postulate the existence of a force actively tending towards death and also a form of *cell suicide*. Every living organism carries out its own death through particular genes that come into play when environmental conditions become unfavourable or the pre-programmed number of cell multiplication has been completed.

William R. Clark (1996), a well-known molecular biologist, claims that the impulse towards self-annihilation is a by-product of the shift to a form of reproduction of the living matter by means of sexual mating. Ordinarily the *genes of death* remain inactive in the open genomes of the germinal cells. As the process of cell differentiation moves forward, the genes that repress death are deactivated. In other words, growth is indissolubly linked to death.

Jean-Claude Ameisen (1999), author of a good book on this very theme, says:

> For a long time it was thought that the death of our cells, like our own death as individuals, could result from accidents and destruction, or from wear and tear, from environmental aggressions and the passage of time, from an ultimate incapacity of any living entity to survive over a given period and over given circumstances (. . .)
>
> Today we know that all of our cells have, at any given moment, the capacity to destroy themselves in a few hours by triggering an endogenous programme of cell suicide. And their daily survival continuously depends on their capacity to perceive signals from the other cells in our body, which alone allow them to repress the onset of their own suicide.
>
> In other words, this means that a cell has lived for one hour, one day, or one month in our body by repressing self-destruction, conversely, this means that most, if not all the dozens of billions of cells that disappear every day in our body, do so in a premature way; they die 'before their time', before any intrinsic and ultimate capacity to survive. It is through information contained in our genes that our cells permanently produce the 'executioners' capable of triggering self-destruction, and the 'protectors', capable of repressing the executioners for as long as our cells will survive.
>
> In a counterintuitive manner, a positive event – life – seems to result from continuous negation of a negative event – self-destruction.

Ameisen's book bears the subtitle *Cell Suicide and Creative Death*, to show the intricate relationship between self-annihilation and the creation of new forms of life, which echoes Freud's thought: "Every living being dies for internal reasons." (5) Thus even biology confirms the indissoluble link between life and death. This is the state that Freud defines as *fusion* of the two instincts and it is the only condition able to preserve, in the living matter as well as in the psyche, the necessary equilibrium between the reasons of life and those of self-destruction.

These recent intuitions of cell biology, though fascinating and unexpectedly in agreement with the Freudian postulates of 1920, cannot, however, be employed to validate the existence of the death instinct, which operates besides the life instinct. Indeed, modern biological research tells us that pre-programmed death is a process activated when the conditions for cell survival no longer obtain and a marked deterioration of the environment makes the continuity of life impossible. This is analogous to what happens on a psychic level: it is, in fact, possible that in our mental life, as well, there might be a pre-disposition to actively seek death, through the activation of self-destructive mechanisms potentially present in all of us, when living is felt to be intolerable. In human creatures, a pre-disposed death would become operative as a result of early and extended traumas, which interfere with psychic survival, because of the intense pain elicited by feeling alive. The earlier the trauma and the more compromised the vital functions, the more self-destructive mechanisms, ready to act at a later time, develop. It is possible, in fact, that traumatic experiences, destined to trigger self-destructive mechanisms, operate at such an early phase – and at a developmental stage when there is no capacity for self-reflection or communicative language – that these traumas remain unconscious and the person who suffered them is unaware of them. Therefore the silent nature of the death instinct would not be the expression of a constitutional disposition, but would rather indicate an early incorporation of a traumatic experience lodged in the unconscious memory and in that part of the person's history unavailable for conscious recall. (6)

NOTES

(1) Many analysts have interpreted Freud very literally. I recall how Cesare Musatti, when already very old, one evening commented before the colleagues of the Milan Centre of Psychoanalysis a dream of his, in which his older brother, who had died young, beckoned him: "Come! Come!" and he replied: "No, I will not come!" Musatti interpreted his dream as a manifestation of a fraternal conflict, rather than as a premonition of death.

(2) Actually, sometimes Freud talked about unconscious representation of death. For instance. In "The Theme of the Three Caskets" (1913) he sees the third female figure as a symbol of death. Having to choose among three Goddesses, people turn to the goddess of Love, who, in reality, is a disguise of the Goddess of death. Freud writes: "Whilst in real life we are necessarily compelled to comply with death, here, transforming Death into the Goddess of Love, we choose."

(3) Similarly, children whose parents are severely depressed or perceived as damaged, inhibit their own lively development in order not to face the guilt for having neglected or abandoned their love objects, when growing up.

(4) The protagonist of Balzac's novel makes an agreement with the devil and receives the skin of a donkey, magical but deadly, in exchange for his own. In fact, this skin has the capacity to fulfil all his wishes, but it shrivels as it accomplishes its magical powers.

(5) The orientations of contemporary biologists confirm August Weissman's intuition. He was a biologist who, towards the end of the nineteenth century, affirmed that the characteristic of aging might have emerged when unicellular organisms had become multicellular and might have stemmed from the differentiation that allows cells to forms individual bodies.

(6) With regard to the quality and the vicissitudes of the strategies towards psychic self-annihilation, I refer the reader back to chapter 4.

17

MELANIE KLEIN AND INNATE DESTRUCTIVENESS

Mors immortalis occidit. (Immortal death kills).
Pier Damiani

Man, the only living being who has a horror of
death, is at the same time the only being who
puts his fellow creatures to death and seeks death.
Edgard Morin

Melanie Klein explicitly contradicts Freud's views on the absence of representation of death in the unconscious, and she states (1948):

> I do not share this view simply because my analytic observations show that there is in the unconscious the fear of annihilation of life. (. . .) Since the struggle between the life and the death instincts persists throughout life, this source of anxiety is never eliminated and enters as a perpetual factor in all anxiety –situations. Anxiety has its origin in the fear of death.

Joan Riviere (1955), Melanie Klein's colleague and collaborator, puts forward an even more radical idea:

We cannot escape the conclusion that an intense fear of death by active aggression or passive neglect is a fundamental element of our emotional life, is as deeply rooted in our unconscious mind as life itself, and it is barricaded off from our conscious experience by every known mechanism of defence.

Whilst for Freud the death instinct is a biological entity, which works within the organism, but has no unconscious representation, for Klein it is a psychic perception, present in the earliest unconscious phantasies. The anxiety experienced by the newborn baby is a direct derivative of the fear of death, activated by the death instinct. Klein maintains that the baby attributes its discomfort and pain to hostile and persecutory forces. To protect itself from this fear, the baby introjects a good breast, which allows it to counteract the perception of a bad and starving breast. This first good internal object, a focal point for ego structuring, facilitates the infant's cohesion and integration:

> Projection, as Freud described, originates from the deflection of the death instinct outwards and in my view it helps the ego to overcome anxiety by ridding it of danger and badness. Introjection of the good object is also used by the ego as a defence against anxiety.

Unlike Freud, Klein thinks that the unconscious contains a representation of death, which coincides with the representation of bad and persecutory objects. The primitive super-ego, which in the internal world threatens the infant with death, would thus constitute one of the earliest representations of the death instinct. The bad objects, left unmodified, would produce the experience of inner death.

Klein introduced a new theoretical perspective, suggesting that the encounter with death is a very early and unavoidable experience and this has widened the horizon of psychoanalytic thinking.

In a passage from her paper "On Identification" (1955), Klein states very clearly that the capacity to face death is closely linked to the state of the internal world of the individual. The fear of death increases noticeably when this is felt to be an attack by the hostile internal objects or when depressive anxiety prevails, thus colouring the perception of the good internal objects, seen as destroyed by malevolent internal figures. When this internal scenario obtains, the inescapable anxiety of fragmentation, loneliness and abandonment, which characterise the beginnings of our psychic functioning, re-emerge cyclically in the course of life. For this reason, the fear of death can be unconsciously likened to the state of agony and chaos in the internal world. In conclusion, the more the person's internal world is peopled by good objects, the more the thought of one's own death can arouse regret and sadness, but not fear of chaos, agony and nameless dread.

Conversely, when splitting or fragmenting processes predominate, persecutory anxiety inevitably becomes so overwhelming as to flood the psychic apparatus and destroy mental well-being. Therefore the intense mental suffering which some people experience on their deathbed could be a revival of their infantile psychotic anxieties.

Klein suggests that our internal object relations interwoven with affects linked to the life instinct, such as love and gratitude, help to protect us from the anxiety of death. Conversely, the pathological structures deriving from the death instinct, in the guise of envy or pathological narcissism foster mistrust and persecution. They are bound to increase the internal threat posed by the fear of death.

BIBLIOGRAPHY

Abadi M., (1984)"Sulla morte: note psicoanalitiche su una fantasia chiave", in Chiavicchia Scalamonti.
Abraham K.,:
—(1911), "Giovanni Segantini: un saggio psicoanalitico" in "*Opere*" vol.II. Torino: Boringhieri.
—(1919), "The Applicability of Psycho-Analytic Treatment to Patients at an Advanced Age", in *Selected Papers on Psychoanalysis*. London: Maresfield Library, (1988).
—(1924), "A Short Study of the Development of the Libido, Viewed in the Light of Mental Disorders", in *Selected Papers on Psychoanalysis*.
Alexander F., (1951), "Buddhist Training as an Artificial Catatonia", *Psychoanal. Rev.*, vol. 18, 129-45.
Ameisen J-C., (1999), *Al cuore della vita. Il suicidio cellulare e la morte creatrice*, Milano: Feltrinelli, (2001).
Améry J., (1988), *Rivolta e rassegnazione. Sull'invecchiare*, Torino: Bollati Boringhieri.
Ariès P., (1979), *The Hour of Our Death*, New York: Random House.
Asimov I., (1992), *The Positronic Man*, Gollancz, U.K.
Barale F., (1982), "Lutto, funzione simbolica e atteggiamento medico verso il morente", *Arch. Psicol. Neurol. Psichiat.*, vol 43, N 2, 254-61.
Bateson G., ed., (1961), *Perceval's Narrative: a Patient's Account of his Psychosys*, Palo Alto: Stanford Uni. Press.
Bauman Z., (1992), *Mortality, Immortality and Other Life Strategies*, Cambridge: Int. University Press.
Becker E., (1973), *The Denial of Death*, London: Free Press, (1977).

Bègoin J., (1989), "La violence du dèsespoir, ou le contresens d'une « pulsion de mort » en psychanalyse", *Rev. Fr. Psychanal.*, vol. 2.

Bergonzi M., (2001),'Riflessioni sulla morte nell'India religiosa', in Crozzoli Aite

Bion W. R., (1962), *Learning from Experience*, London: Maresfield Library, (1984).

—(1970), *Attention and Interpretation*, London: Maresfield Library, (1984).

Bollas, C., (1989), *Forces of Destiny*, London: FAB.

Bonasia E., (1988) "Pulsione di morte o terrore di morire? Una ricerca sul problema della morte in psicoanalisi", in *Riv. Psicoanal.*, vol. 34, N.2.

Bordi S., (1968), "Sulla fugacità (una nota sul processo creativo)", *Psiche*, vol.5, N.1-2-3-4.

Cavicchia Scalamonti A. (ed.), (1984), *Il 'senso' della morte. Contributi per una sociologia della morte*, Napoli, Liguori.

Chasseguet-Smirgel J., (1986), *I due alberi del giardino: saggi psicoanalitici sul ruolo del padre e della madre nel sistema psichico*, Milano, Feltrinelli, (1991).

Clark R. W., (1998), *Sex and the Origin of Death*, Oxford: Int. Uni. Press.

Cohen N. A., (1982), "On Loneliness and the Aging Process", *Int. J. Psicho-Anal.*, vol.63, 149-56.

Coltart N., (1991), "The Analysis of an Elderly Patient", *Int. J. Psicho-Ana.l*, vol.72, 209-19.

Crozzoli Aite L., (ed.), (2001) *Sarà così lasciare la vita*, Roma: Paoline Editoriali Libri.

Davies J. M., (1996), "Dissociation, Repression and Reality Testing in the Countertransference : the Controversy over Memory and False Memory in the Psychoanalytic Treatment of Adult Sorvivors of Childhood Sexual Abuse", *Psychoanal. Dial.*, vol.6, N.2.

Davis M.& Wallbridge D. C., (1981), *Boundary and Space: An Introduction to the Work of D. W. Winnicott*, New York: Brunner-Mazel. (Revised edition London: Karnac Books 1991).

De Masi, F., (1996), "Strategie psichiche verso l'autoannientamento psichico", *Riv. Psicoanal.*, vol.44, 549-66.

—(2000),"L'inconscio: prospettive attuali", *Quad. Centro mil. Psicoanal. C. Musatti*, N.4.
—(2001), "Considerazioni sulla terapia psicoanalitica della psicosi: in margine ad un articolo di Pier Luigi Rossi", *Riv. Psicoanal.*, vol.47, N.1.
Edelman G. M., (1992), *Bright Air, Brilliant Fire: On the Matter of the Mind*, New York: Int. University Press.
Eigen M., (1996), *Psychic Deadness*, Northvale New Jersey London: Jason Arons.
Elias N., (1982), *La solitudine del morente*, Bologna: Il Mulino (1985).
Epstein M., (1990), "Beyond the Oceanic Feeling: Psychoanalytic Study of Buddhist Meditation", *Int. Rev. Psycho-Anal.*, vol.17, 159-66.
Fachinelli E., (1983), *Claustrofilia*, Milano: Adelphi.
Fenichel E., (1946), *The Psycho-Analytic Theory of Neurosis*, London: Routledge.
Freud S., (1903), *Freud's Psycho-Analytic Procedure*, S.E. VII.
—(1904), *On Psychotherapy*, S.E. VII.
—(1911), *Formulations on the Two Principles of Mental Functioning*, S.E. XII.
—(1913), *The Theme of the Three Caskets*, S.E. XII.
—(1915a), *On Transience*, S.E. XIV.
—(1915b), *Instincts and Their Vicissitudes*, S.E. XIV.
—(1915c), *Mourning and Melancholia*, S.E. XIV.
—(1915d), *Thoughts for the Times on War and Death*, S.E. XIV.
—(1920), *Beyond the Pleasure Principle*, S. E. XVIII.
—(1922), *The Ego and the Id*, S.E.XIX.
—(1925), *Inhibitions, Symptoms an Anxiety*, S. E. XX.
—(1931), *Female Sexuality*, S. E. XXI.
—(1937), *Analysis Terminable and Interminable*, S. E. XXIII.
Gadamer H. G., (1993), *Dove si nasconde la salute*, Milano: Cortina, (1994).
Garland C., (ed), (1998a), *Understanding Trauma. A Psychoanalytic Approach*, London: Karnac Books, (2002).
—(1998b) "Thinking About the Trauma", in Garland (1998a)
Green A. et al, (1986), "La pulsion de mort", First EPF Symposium, Marseille

Guzzi M., (2001), "La morte si sta avvicinando", in Crozzoli Aite.
Hinze E., (1987), "Transference and Countertransference in the Psychoanalytic Treatment of Older Patients", *Int. Rev. Psycho-Anal.*, vol. 14, 465-74.
Horton P. C., (1974), "The Mystical Experience: Substance of an Illusion", *J. Amer. Psychoanal. Ass.*, vol. 22, 364-79.
Jacques E., (1965), "Death and the Mid-Life Crisis", *Int. J. Psycho-Anal.*, vol. 46, 502-14.
Jankélévitch V., (1994), *Pensare la morte?*, Milano: Cortina, (1995).
King P., (1974), "Notes on the Psychoanalysis of Older Patients. Reappraisal of the Potentialities for Change during the Second Half of Life", *J. Anal. Psychol.*, vol. 19, 22-37.
—(1980), "The Life Cycle as Indicated by the Nature of the Transference in the Psychoanalysis of the Middle-Aged Elderly", *Int. J. Psycho-Anal.*, vol. 61, 153-60.
Klein M., (1932), *The Psycho-Analysis of Children*, London: The Hogarth Press.
—(1946), "Notes on Some Schizoid Mechanisms", in *Envy and Gratitude, and Other Works: 1946-1963*, London: The Hogarth Press, (1975).
—(1948), "On the Theory of Anxiety and Guilt" in Klein (1975).
—(1955), "On Identification", in Klein (1975).
—(1963), "On the Sense of Loneliness", in Klein (1975).
—*Scritti 1921-1958*, Torino: Boringhieri, (1978).
Klein M., Heimann P., and Money-Kyrle R.E., (eds.), (1955), *New Directions in Psychoanalysis*, London: Tavistock Publications; in paperback, Tavistock Publications (1971).
Landsberg P. L., (1936), *Essais sur l'expérience de la mort*, Paris: Desclée de Brouwer.
Le Doux J., (1996), *Il cervello emotivo. Alle origini delle emozioni*, Milano: Baldini & Castoldi, (1998).
Lock W., (1982), "Comments on Dr. Norman A. Cohen's Paper: 'On Loneliness and the Aging Process", *Int. J. Psycho-Anal.*, vol. 63.
London J., (1909), *Martin Eden*, London: Penguin Books, (1994)
Morin E., (1970), *L'uomo e la morte*, Roma: Meltemi, (2002).

Nietzsche F., (1884), *Considerazioni inattuali*, Milano: Adelphi, (1972).
Phillips A., (1999), *Darwin's Worms*, London: Faber & Faber.
Plato, *Complete Works by Plato*, Huckett Pub. Co., (1997).
Pollock G. H., (1982), "On Aging and Psychopathology", *Int. J. Psycho-Anal.*, vol. 63, 275-81.
Riviere J., "General Introduction to Melanie Klein, Paula Heimann, Susan Isaacs, and Joan Riviere, Developments in Psycho-Analysis" in *The Inner World of Joan Riviere. Collected Papers 1920-1958*, London: Karnac Books, (1991).
Rosenfeld H., (1971) "A Clinical Approach to the Psychoanalytic Theory of Life and Death Instincts. An Investigation into the Aggressive Aspects of Narcissism", *Int. J. Psycho-Anal.*, vol. 52, 168-178.
—(1978), "Notes on the Psychopathology and Psychoanalytic Treatment of Some Borderline Patients", *Int. J. Psycho-Anal.*, vol. 58, 215-23. Paper given at the First EPF Symposium, in Green et al. (1986).
Scheler M., (1984), "Morte e sopravvivenza" in Cavicchia Scalamonti.
Schur M., (1972), *Freud Living and Dying*, New York: Int. Uni. Press, (1974).
Schnitzler A., (1892), *Morire*, Milano: Mondadori, (1988).
Searles H. F., (1961), "Schizophrenia and the Inevitability of Death", *Psychiat. Q.*, vol. 35, 361-65.
—(1965), *Collected Papers on Schizophrenia and Related Subjects*, London: The Hogarth Press and The Institute of Psychoanalysis.
Segal H., (1958), "Fear of Death and the Analysis of an Old Man", *Int. J. Psycho-Anal.*, vol. 39, 178-82.
—(1993), "On the Clinical Usefulness of the Concept of the Death Instinct", *Int. J. Psycho-Anal.*, vol. 74, 55-63.
Sofsky W., (1996), *Il paradiso della crudeltà*, Torino: Einaudi, (2001).
Spagnoli A., (1995), "... *e divento sempre più vecchio". Jung, Freud, la psicologia del profondo e l'invecchiamento*, Torino: Bollati Boringhieri.

Thomas L. V., (1975), *Antropologia della morte*, Milano: Garzanti, (1976).
Tolstoy L., *La morte di Ivàn I'lic*, Milano: Mondatori, (1991).
Wilie H. V. and Wilie M. L., (1987), "The Older Analysand: Countertransference Issues in Psychoanalysis", *Int. J. Psycho-Anal.*, vol. 68, 343-51.
Winnicott D. W., (1958), *The Family and Individual Development*, London: Tavistock Publications, (1965).
—(1971), *Playing and Reality*, London: Tavistock Publications.

INDEX OF NAMES

Abadi, M. 118
Abraham, Karl 16, 52, 73, 99–100, 134–135, 140
Alexander, F 57
Ameisen, Jean-Claude 143
Amery, Jean 35
Asimov, Isaac 27

Balzac, H. de 142, 145
Barale, F. 38
Bateson, Gregory 107
Bauman, Z. 38, 122
Becker, E. 38
Bègoin, G. 61
Bergonzi, M. 27
Bettini, Giovanna 126
Bion, W. R. 17, 47, 114
Bollas, Christopher 12, 72, 73
Bonasia, Emanuele 66
Bordi, Sergio 32–33

Chasseguet-Smirgel, Janine 57
Clark, William R. 142
Cohen, N. A. 101
Coltart, Nina 98, 101

Darwin, C. 14
Davies, J. M. 114

Edelman, G. M. 12, 25, 77–78
Eden, Martin 16
Eigen, Michael 66
Epstein, M. 57

Fachinelli, Elvio 126
Fraiberg, S. 18
Freud, Sigmund 11, 14–15, 18, 21–22, 26, 31, 48, 53, 57-59, 66, 72–75, 97-98, 100–101, 106, 110, 112-113, 116, 126, 130-134, 136–141, 145, 147
Freud, Ernst 32

Gadamer, H. G. 37
Garland, Caroline 113
Guzzi, Marco 38

Heidegger, Martin 67–68
Hinze, E. 101
Horton, P. C. 59
Husserl, E. 22

Jacques, Elliot 12, 86–87
Jankélévitch, V. 35
Jaspers, Karl 122

King, Pearl 100–101
Klein, Melanie 11, 12, 16, 26, 53, 66, 70, 86, 100, 107–108, 116, 120, 146–147
Kohut, H. 18

Landsberg, P. L. 108
Le Doux, J. 114, 118
London, Jack 49–50

Morin, Edgard 36, 69, 110

INDEX

Musatti, Cesare 144

Nietzsche, F. 77

Phillips, Adam 141
Pollock, G. H. 101

Rilke, Rainer Maria 31–32, 133
Riviere, Joan 146
Rosenfeld, H. 17, 19, 54, 60

Salomé, Lou Andreas 32
Scheler, M. 37
Schnitzler, Arthur 126
Searles, Harold 22, 23, 104, 108–109, 115

Segal, Hanna 58–59, 101, 102
Segantini, G. 16, 52–53
Socrates 68
Sofsky, W. 111
Spagnoli, Alberto 119

Tolstoy, L. 12, 81, 85
Tustin 18

Weissman, August 145
Wilie, Harold 98, 101
Wilie, Mavis 98, 101
Winnicott 11, 12, 16, 18, 25, 47, 54, 70–73, 74, 76, 120